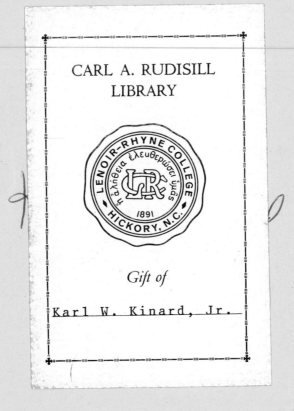

OXFORD MONOGRAPHS ON MUSIC

❦

NORTH ITALIAN CHURCH MUSIC
IN THE AGE OF MONTEVERDI

NORTH ITALIAN CHURCH MUSIC

IN THE

AGE OF MONTEVERDI

JEROME ROCHE

CLARENDON PRESS · OXFORD
1984

Oxford University Press, Walton Street, Oxford OX2 6DP
London New York Toronto
Delhi Bombay Calcutta Madras Karachi
Kuala Lumpur Singapore Hong Kong Tokyo
Nairobi Dar es Salaam Cape Town
Melbourne Auckland

and associated companies in
Beirut Berlin Ibadan Mexico City Nicosia

Oxford is a trade mark of Oxford University Press

Published in the United States
by Oxford University Press, New York

British Library Cataloguing in Publication Data
Roche, Jerome.
North Italian church music in the age of Monteverdi
1. Church music—Italy—History and criticism
2. Music—Italy—History
and criticism—17th century
I. Title
783'02'6   ML2933
ISBN 0-19-316118-4

Library of Congress Cataloging in Publication Data
Roche, Jerome.
North Italian church music in the age of Monteverdi.
Bibliography: p
1. Church music—Italy—17th century—History and criticism.
2. Church music—Catholic Church—History and criticism.
I. Title
ML2933.R6   1984   783'.02'6245   83-17456
ISBN 0-19-316118-4

Set by Wyvern Typesetting Limited, Bristol
Printed in Great Britain
by The Thetford Press,
Thetford, Norfolk

In memory of my Parents

LAURENCE ROCHE 1891–1968

MARIA ROCHE 1900–1968

Contents

Abbreviations

CM∭Mꝃ

S, A, T, B	Soprano, Alto, Tenor, Bass
RISM (+ date)	*Répertoire international des sources musicales: Recueils Imprimés, XVIe–XVIIe siècles* (Munich/Duisburg, 1960).

In Musical Examples

Bar.	Baritone
bc	Basso continuo
Ch.	Choir
Ct.	Cornett
Trb.	Trombone
Vln.	Violin

In Notes and Bibliography

AcM	Acta Musicologica
AnMc	Analecta Musicologica
AMw	Archiv für Musikwissenschaft
GSJ	Galpin Society Journal
JAMS	Journal of the American Musicological Society
KJb	Kirchenmusikalisches Jahrbuch
MMg	Monatshefte für Musikgeschichte
MD	Musica Disciplina
ML	Music and Letters
MQ	Musical Quarterly
MR	Music Review
MT	Musical Times
NA	Note d'Archivio per la storia musicale
PRMA	Proceedings of the Royal Musical Association
RIM	Rivista italiana di musicologia
RMI	Rivista musicale italiana
RMARC	R. M. A. Research Chronicle
SMw	Studien zur Musikwissenschaft
ZMw	Zeitschrift für Musikwissenschaft

Clef Notation

G2 C1 C2 C3 C4 F3 F4

Books, dissertations, and articles are identified in *footnotes* by author and abbreviated title. Full details are listed in the bibliography. Psalm numberings are those in the Vulgate.

Preface

CRITICAL

THIS book represents a thorough revision of my doctoral dissertation, entitled 'North Italian Liturgical Music in the Early Seventeenth Century'. Inasmuch as it is concerned with music written first and foremost for church services, its scope remains the same as that of the dissertation in excluding both oratorio and sacred madrigal; so too does the geographical region surveyed, for northern Italy as an entity was in the forefront of musical developments in the early baroque period, and church music in Rome was – for a time at least – less influential and less mainstream.

My decision to cover such a large geographical area was deliberate, for my aim has been to give an overall view of church music activity not restricted to any one city. Until Giovanni Gabrieli's death in 1612, Venice had been the hub of such activity; but after that there was no one 'school' of composers, no one city acting as fountainhead in the way Florence did for early opera. Venice proved to be no more the arbiter of church style than did her most illustrious composer, Monteverdi. New lines of development could, and did, spring up in whatever city or town the composer that pioneered them happened to be working. Sociological, economic, and political factors affected different cities in different ways. A study of church music in Venice or any other single city alone might present a fascinating microcosm, but it would not enable us to gain the wider perspective that we need in order to appreciate the relative position of Venice and her music in such a thriving area during such an important period of musical development.

The 'age of Monteverdi' is to be understood as the period of that composer's mature working life – from about 1605 onwards: a chronological timespan which neatly comprises the years of foundation and development in seventeenth-century Italian church music as a whole. His death in 1643 marks a convenient signing-off point, for by the mid-1640s the years of experiment were largely at an end, and mid-baroque tendencies in musical taste and style were becoming apparent.

The updating of knowledge represented in this book was to some extent the fruit of my preparing articles on many of the composers mentioned for *The New Grove Dictionary of Music and Musicians* (20 vols., London, 1980). With the latter's appearance, composer entries by other scholars and articles on Italian cities have yielded new information, which I have incorporated where appropriate. Since *The New Grove* contains conveniently arranged biographical information and lists of works for each composer, no attempt has been made to duplicate such material here except in so far as biographical data can be presented as part of the geographical, city-by-city survey in Chapter II. I have also taken account of two recent important studies by Kurtzman and Moore, concerning respectively the Monteverdi Vespers, and Vespers at St. Mark's in Venice. Sadly, Whenham's useful study of the secular repertory of concertato duet and dialogue appeared too late to affect my consideration of its sacred counterpart in Chapter V.

Only a very small proportion of the music discussed in Chapters V–VIII, which deal with musical style, is available in modern editions; the exceptions are the works of Giovanni Gabrieli and Monteverdi. Italian music has had no share in the systematic publication of collected works, or even selected works and anthologies, in critical modern editions, and the situation is bleak indeed by comparison with that of English, German, and Austrian music of the period. No apology is therefore offered for the fact that the musical illustrations to these chapters are more extensive than might otherwise be expected. Even so, the examples cannot by themselves convey the overall impact of a work as a whole, nor such things as the subtleties of its structure. What is needed – and the sooner, the better – is the publication of a body of this music in a modern edition, not only to compensate for the present lack of material but also to encourage the discovery of its attractions in performance.

My most grateful thanks are due to the librarians of many libraries in Italy, England, and Germany – above all, those at the Civico Museo Bibliografico Musicale in Bologna and at the Fondazione Giorgio Cini in Venice – for allowing me facilities to study original sources and microfilms; to the late Monsignor Angelo Meli, who originally brought the archives at S. Maria Maggiore in Bergamo to my attention and gave me the freedom of them; to the Italian Government, the Department of Education and Science, the Research Fund of the University of Durham, and the Fondazione Giorgio Cini in Venice, for financial support; to David Munrow (among others) for bringing some of this music to a larger public through performances and a recording; to my wife, an invaluable amanuensis whether in helping me transcribe music, suggesting improvements to my text, or undertaking the heroic task of typing the final copy of this book; to David Fallows, of the University of Manchester, for reading through, checking, and making many helpful comments on one of its drafts; and last, to Professor Denis Arnold, who was my guiding light throughout the earlier years of my research, and who has never ceased to give me invaluable advice and help.

Durham University　　　　　　　　　　　　　　　　　　JEROME ROCHE
January 1983

Introduction

THE Monteverdi quatercentenary in 1967 concentrated wonderfully the minds of many in the musical world, for it helped to make Monteverdi's whole output accessible and open to fresh critical assessment. In the years that followed, the church music benefited especially; the old squabbles about the Vespers of 1610 were forgotten in the face, on the one hand, of new historical research, and on the other, of a spate of new recordings – not only of that work but also of many of his later, Venetian compositions. It was at last possible to hear a wide variety of sacred music written in the early Baroque by one Italian composer, and to appreciate the range of musical forces it involved – from a simple solo motet with continuo to a huge, showy work for a special occasion like the *Gloria a7*. For the first time, the stylistic dichotomies in Monteverdi's sacred music could be perceived in sound – the struggle between old and new techniques in the Vespers of 1610,(1) the gropings towards a convincing 'old style' based on Renaissance(2) polyphony in the three Mass settings; and (by contrast) the assured handling(3) of idomatic writing and musical structure in the mature Venetian psalms and motets.

But the very accessibility of the sacred music of one isolated genius must still leave us in the dark about his true historical position. For an estimate of that, we need to know a lot more about the sacred music of his Italian contemporaries – what it was like, and what impulses brought it into being. Though the Monteverdi revival was timely in that it to some extent excited interest in the general musical background of the period, it is quite unnecessary to justify the present study of his contemporaries merely on account of his own pre-eminent position. Many of the church composers of northern Italy were capable of writing excellent music in their own right, and independently of any influence he may have wielded; they need not creep into the public gaze under his coat tails, so to speak. The early Baroque in northern Italy was one of those periods that combined the volatility of change and experiment in musical style with an exceptional intensity of activity in the publication and wide dissemination of music – above all church music, which was ousting the madrigal as the foundation of the printing houses' commercial prosperity. For once, the result was a repertory which as a whole seems more than usually capable of rising above the level of the mediocre, composed by men (and women) who more often than not deserve the label *Kleinmeister* in the most positive sense of that term. This is not a brash claim provided we judge the music by what it set out to achieve, given the state of the musical language of the time. Thus we should not regret its limitations simply because it lacks the greater harmonic variety of later baroque music (on that pretext much of Monteverdi must also fail to please), and less still because it speaks to us with less immediacy than more recent and therefore familiar music (we do not expect a Monteverdi opera to sound like one by Verdi). In fact, the simple sincerity and fervour of much of this church music may well have a greater immediacy to the listener today than either the disembodied, other-worldly feeling of Renaissance polyphony on the one hand or the contrived, all-too-worldly, and liturgically irrelevant church music of some later epochs – but that is a subjective viewpoint.

What, then, is early baroque church music in northern Italy like? Let us examine the 'stylistic continuum' in order not to be at sea once the discussion begins to focus on musical style. The first point to be made is that we are dealing with the earliest period in musical history when a new style (*stile moderno*) and an old style (*stile antico*) begin to coexist in church music. But most composers preferred to write most of their church music in the up-to-date idiom – which may surprise those who tend to consider the Church as a reactionary force. The bulk of old-style music was written either in a post-Palestrina idiom, as seen in the work of north Italians like Asola, Croce, and Viadana, or in the double-choir manner of a composer like Andrea Gabrieli. We may therefore concentrate on the new so-called concertato style. Here the fundamental factor was the emancipation of the organ *basso continuo*, whereby the voice parts were freed from the need to be self-sufficient; a feature ubiquitous in all the church music we shall be discussing (even old-style music was issued with a *basso per l'organo*, as they called it, for the purposes of accompaniment).

This led to the great popularity with composers of the concertato duet, solo, and trio textures (in that order) over a continuo bass, dealt with in the first part of Chapter V. The solo motet was of course akin to secular monody in principle, though in practice it presented a freer mixture of what may be regarded as recitative and *arioso* styles than the distinct types of solo madrigal (recitative-like, declamatory) and aria (tuneful, faster bass line, often triple time). The duet, though sometimes conceived as a dialogue between two voices in a semi-dramatic manner, was more usually an ensemble piece often for equal voices (two sopranos or tenors) over a free bass line; the voices would sing in mellifluous thirds but there was also plenty of contrapuntal interplay and even canonic writing, which, together with the frequent dissonances between two close-lying voice parts, created the abundant tension typical of all concertato music. Excellent results could be achieved by these simple means; vocal display was not the point, and was better sought in the solo pieces. There can be few more appealing examples of the genre than the two Grandi duets *Hodie nobis de caelo* and *Anima Christi*,[1] the first of which also has the kind of well-thought-out formal structure sometimes encountered even in small-scale works. The second has no need of this, for its text invites freer treatment. As for the three-voice texture, often this was like a duet with the bass line 'vocalized', with ornaments to render it more singable, though occasionally we find trios for three equal sopranos or even SST over the continuo (as in Giovanni Battista Crivelli's *Quando te videbo* of 1626). A glance at all this music will show how the time signature usually changes to triple at some point in a motet, the idiom becoming more tuneful and less declamatory, either for simple variety's sake or in response to the words.

The advent of the *basso continuo* also enabled composers to explore a whole new range of contrasts of sonority as, for example, those between solo voices and instruments, and it was not long before the instrumentalists who played regularly in church were integrated with solo singers in a new kind of sacred chamber music, much more intimate than the grand ceremonial manner of Giovanni Gabrieli's last years in Venice. Grandi proved a pioneer in this field, and the interesting possibilities of a pair of equal voices and violins over the continuo can be seen in a motet like *Bone Jesu verbum Patris* (see Ex. 20, p. 85–6). This kind of texture was equally favoured for secular music, and can be found in some of Monteverdi's later madrigals – *Chiome d'oro* from Book VII, for instance.

At the same time, the principle of independent vocal lines over a harmony-implying continuo part infused a new lease of life into the more conventional four- to six-part textures. Here the polarity of the so-called 'melody and bass' layout of monody or trio sonata was less in evidence, for although a new sense of harmonic progression underlaid the musical argument, counterpoint was by no means abandoned, and in some stylistically cautious music the vocal texture was rich enough for the continuo to be almost superfluous. Such music was, however, no less expressive for that, and derived its idiom from the unaccompanied Italian madrigal of Monteverdi's early years; an excellent example of this is Grandi's motet *Versa est in luctum* (see Ex. 23, p. 91). The five-part scoring in this work is typical, and led, in more continuo-oriented music, to fragmentation into concertato strands of upper and lower duets and bass (e.g. SS/AT/B or SS/TT/B) which could be contrasted with the full tutti. Another 'modern' scheme, most appropriate in a work for SATB, was to have self-contained solos for each voice separated by tuttis, perhaps set to the same music by way of refrain. The more diverse the scoring, the more attractive the idea of a coherent structural scheme became to some composers, and we shall at times be dwelling upon this fascinating experimentation in compositional logic. Of course, the need for it was not as pressing as in abstract intrumental music which lacked the prop of a text. A great many motets succeed despite having no formal organization, because their texts do not call for it; in those most dependent on changes of mood it would indeed be inimical. There is, after all, no point in looking for abstract structural logic in the genre most dependent of all on words, the Italian madrigal, where often the only musical repetitions are to be found in schemes like *ABB*, which may well be inspired by a composer's wish to stress a particular part of the text.

Questions of abstract formal organization loom largest in large-scale Italian church music, most of which consisted of settings of the Mass and of Vesper psalms, often to long texts laid down for the principal liturgical rites. The very length and diffuseness of the texts invited the more varied music that could be created with larger forces, and there was a need to compensate for this diversity by imposing some kind of musical design to knit all the elements together. In Chapters VII and VIII, which deal with music in seven and more parts, we shall again be charting the growth of this tendency. As for the music itself, there are basically two kinds under this heading: the more conventional is that for polychoral scorings, though even this gradually acquired a 'new look' and came close to what we would recognize as a concerto grosso scheme, with solo and ripieno choirs; more progressive is the so-called 'mixed concertato' style which, instead of having spatially separated groups, resembles the few voiced style writ large, with freely mixing groups of small vocal and instrumental textures (often in pairs of equal voices and instruments, e.g. SS/TT/BB, two violins) welded together by occasional massive homophonic tuttis, perhaps reinforced by extra voices or trombones. Classic examples of this practice are found in Monteverdi's *Gloria a7*, and Giovanni Antonio Rigatti's Magnificat (see Ex. 40, p. 139).

So much for the wide range of performing resources and scorings that we find in this church music. As a body of works, a repertory, it is really more unified than this range may have led us to suppose. One of its principal features is reliance upon the art of melody. The emancipation of this element in music is of course attributable to the rise of the continuo and to new modes of singing, but it needs stressing that a composer often achieved distinction first and foremost through his capacities as a melodist, for in melody lay the heart of feeling. An illustration of this can be seen in Ex. 10 (p. 68), taken from Bartolomeo Barbarino's *Salve Regina*: the strength of this passage is built up by the skilful use of verbal and musical repetition, not to mention several other more fleeting devices. It comes from a solo motet, a type of piece which must stand or fall by the quality of its melody. But a melodic gift was just as much an asset in more complex textures, for in the Baroque, contrapuntal material often gained by being melodically distinguished in the first place, and even large concertato works were seldom so dense as to drown out a deft melodic turn of phrase. Hand in hand with melody went ornamentation which, in sacred music, was often written in and, if so, was hardly ever very virtuosic in character (the ornamentation in Monteverdi's Vespers is quite uncharacteristic of the written-in variety).

Like the melodic style itself, the ornaments were freshly conceived; they owed much to Caccini and his followers, and were aimed at enhancing the presentation of the words in a declamatory, almost rhetorical manner. But though the music, in emulating the new style of monody and the early opera, might employ means that approach the theatrical – especially when contrasted with the polyphony of the previous century, or its remnants in the *stile antico* – it never lost sight of sincere religious feeling, or at least of liturgical propriety; the total lack of vapid display for its own sake is proof of that. In any case, as most of it was part-music, a modicum of contrapuntal interest was bound to survive, lending rigour to the musical argument and providing an antidote to pure, sensuous expression. In this respect church music stands apart from opera and monody, even though its outlook is firmly progressive rather than traditional.

The great mass of composers of this repertory are but names in a book or encyclopaedia. Who, then, are the heroes of our narrative? Above all, Alessandro Grandi, who was without doubt the most talented church composer of the day in northern Italy. He also contributed to the art of song as a writer of solo cantatas and arias, so it is not surprising that he was a distinguished melodist, and this shows up in all his church music. We shall be encountering his name many times, for he wrote in many of the different genres – solo motets, ensemble works with and without obbligato strings, double-choir pieces, an orchestral Mass. The many contemporary reprints of his motet books show how widely his talent was admired in his day. Then comes Ignazio Donati, whose fascinating career took him to several parts of northern Italy, and who was another outstanding pioneer of the small concertato motet before 1630. Later in date (mainly post-1630) and more centred on Venice were Giovanni Rovetta, Monteverdi's assistant and later successor at St. Mark's, and Giovanni Antonio Rigatti, a truly meteoric talent who died at the age of thirty-four, but whose many excellent psalm settings are original in style and less in thrall to Monteverdi's influence than Rovetta's music usually was. To go beyond these is to run the risk of merely listing names, a temptation that must be resisted at this point. It is to be hoped that the survey of the music will throw sufficient light in turn upon the many talented lesser figures, whose capabilities are by no means to be gauged by the length of their list of works or by the depth of their present-day obscurity. Few, for example, have heard of Rigatti but Viadana will be a name familiar to most students of music around 1600, if only for his *Cento concerti ecclesiastici*. Now Viadana, to be frank, scarcely rises above the level of Tovey's Interesting Historical Figure, whereas it can be argued that some of Rigatti's music is so imaginative and appealing that if we were to credit Monteverdi with its composition, not even the most perceptive critic would raise an eyebrow. Not that such value-judgements are the concern of this book; the music can speak for itself. The primary aim is to place it in a historical perspective.

CHAPTER I

⟪≋⟫

The Climate of Thought Affecting Church Music

IT has often been assumed that the Church, especially the Catholic Church, has always been a force for conservatism, indeed a harbour for the reactionary elements in society. Upon this premise rests a further assumption: that church music and 'progressive' music can never be synonymous, for church music is bound to lag behind the developments of the day. Now the period around 1600 has long been accepted as being of crucial importance for the forging of new trends in musical history – but the prejudices just mentioned have usually excluded from consideration the idea that the church music of the time could have had any role to play in all this change. That church music has not been fully assessed in a dispassionate manner before owes much to overconcentration upon the emergence of a new art-form (the opera) and a New Music (the monody). Earlier this century these twin developments dominated work on early baroque music, and tended to encourage an approach to musical history which treated Renaissance and Baroque as separate compartments. More recently, historical study has shown a greater clarity and perspective first in acknowledging that the roots of opera and monody lie in the theory and practice of the Renaissance, and second by aiding us to appreciate the essentially transitional nature of musical developments between, say, 1570 and 1630. But at the same time, the post-war explosion of studies in Renaissance sacred music, whereby a vast corpus of collected editions has appreared in print, has created a new imbalance in the availability of music that has not helped the cause of the early baroque sacred repertory.

One need not dwell any further on the reasons for the neglect of our subject-matter. But a first stage in approaching it will be to challenge certain common prejudices about the Church by presenting an altogether different view in such a way as to demonstrate points of contact between trends in church history and in church music. We should examine the achievements of the early baroque church composers not by the sole yardstick of Florentine monody but in the light of church art-forms and church history in general, and, later, as the outgrowth of musical tendencies already present in the late Renaissance.

The Church's position as patron of the arts was changing during the later sixteenth century. Wittkower has pointed out how the cultural climate in mid-century Rome was austere, anti-humanist, anti-worldly, and even anti-artistic, owing to the frugalities of court life under popes like Paul IV and Pius V.[1] By the 1580s, during the pontificate of Sixtus V, much had changed; the spirit was a positive rather than a negative one, and the ethos of those times is admirably characterized by Paul Henry Láng, who writes of '. . . the impulse of the religious struggle, Catholic consciousness, warm breath of mysticism, ecstasy, erotic martyrdom . . . a moral refreshment of the Church . . . a new, grandiose spectacular culture . . . a strengthened cult of the saints . . .'[2] Láng here refers to a 'new Catholic art, complete in its allegiance to the Church', observing that the Church was never hostile to art or music that reflected its emotional life. It is this positive spirit that was to nurture, among so many other things, the church music of the early Baroque.

It nurtured other forms of church art, too, like architecture, painting, and sculpture. The characteristic that seems most to connect architecture with music at the end of the sixteenth century is not the calm balance of structure (a Renaissance concept) but the exploitation of space, the contrast of densities; the concentration upon space in so many new churches of the time – the Gesù in Rome, for instance – makes them ideally suited, acoustically as well as aesthetically, to polychoral music.[3] Church painting exploited the idea of space too, for it was the purpose of those vast ceiling frescos to lift the gaze upwards in the direction of heaven in just the same way that music was supposed to uplift the spirit. The self-conscious tricks of the painter, such as the arresting *trompe-l'œil* effects typified by the false dome of S. Ignazio in Rome, were paralleled in music by simple or multiple echo effects, which also deceived the beholder's perception of space. Above all – and this is as true of sculpture as of painting – there was a new sensuousness in church art. Though present before 1600 in the more madrigalian sacred music (especially in that hybrid form the spiritual madrigal), this later characterized a vast number of early baroque Italian motets, making the common label *sacri affetti* quite appropriate.

The Council of Trent and the Counter-Reformation

The historical background to the immediate post-Tridentine period was one of transition from the austere, defensive papacy of the 1560s to the more confident and outward-looking attitudes of the 1580s under Sixtus V. He approved of the progressive movements within the Church, the Jesuits, and the Oratorians, those seemingly opposed offshoots of neo-Catholicism which in reality had much in common. The strength of the papacy's position was aided by the lessening of former dangers, as the Catholic position became consolidated over many parts of Europe.[4]

Though the Council of Trent, which ended in 1563, represented a fresh assessment of the guidelines for church art, it did not assist the Church on the political front, and a conventional authoritarianism remained. The Council failed to reform the power of the Catholic princes, whose unabated absolutism was to reduce the Church's influence in the south of Europe just as the Protestants had diminished it in the north. It made no statements on public or private morality. It did not demand recognition of the Church as an independent society, forfeiting the assurances of protection that would have resulted.[5] The political trend was towards continued temporal power and a high-handed attitude, as when Ferrara was swallowed up as a papal fief in 1598 upon the extinction of the direct male line of the Este dukes, or the Duchy of Urbino annexed in 1631. Temporal princes, like Philip II of Spain, sought to control what reforms there were. The other side of the coin of open-mindedness in the arts was a worldliness and nepotism that showered gold and bestowed social rank upon papal relatives, the spending of fortunes on soirées and spectacles, the commissioning, by a family like the Barberini, of operas, churches, libraries, and the building of monuments, palaces, convents and churches. Only an independently-minded republic like Venice, aided by the efforts of men like Fra Paolo Sarpi, could preserve its freedom in the face of the Church's authoritarian posture.

The effects of the Council of Trent upon churchly art-forms were more salutary, even if its directives were vague. In general, there were three guidelines in the reforms – clarity, simplicity, and intelligibility; realistic interpretation; and an emotional stimulus to piety. Music in particular was discussed at a committee session in October 1562, under the heading 'Abuses in the Sacrifice of the Mass'; the conclusion reached was that music must serve to uplift the faithful, that the words should be intelligible, and that secular expression should be avoided.[6]

In November 1563 the task of implementing these reforms was entrusted to the Provincial Synods, and it is instructive to follow up the application of the Tridentine recommendations by Cardinal Carlo Borromeo, Archbishop of Milan, one of the most powerful leaders of the Counter-Reformation. He had played an important part in the final sessions of the Council and had in 1565 assumed active control of liturgical matters in Milan, prescribing at a Provincial Synod the canon against 'impure' church music (i.e. that based on secular melodies). He was acknowledged as 'the model bishop for the Catholic world of his time, zealous, efficient, ascetic, tireless, charitable, selfless, uncompromising'.[7] The relationship between Borromeo and the composer Vincenzo Ruffo, his *maestro di cappella* in the 1570s, has been the subject of a penetrating study by Lewis Lockwood,[8] who sees in Ruffo's express adoption, in his Masses of 1570, of a syllabic, chordal style that would render the words intelligible, a case of the artist being caught up in institutional changes on the part of his patron, the Church – a patron no longer neutral or lenient, but a militant force. To suggest, as Lockwood does,[9] that such a situation is a distant prefiguration of a twentieth-century one in which authoritarian patronage confronts musical style, is to take too pessimistic a view of the Counter-Reformation Church. While it is true that Ruffo, by subtitling his 1570 Masses 'according to Conciliar decree', furnishes an isolated case of direct response to the Tridentine rulings, it is equally obvious that, though they might never have admitted altering their style as a result of these rulings, many composers – Palestrina most notably – tended to adopt a more syllabic, homophonic approach, especially in Mass settings. In any case, the notion of textual intelligibility was the corollary of a basic sixteenth-century tenet, that the purpose of music was to heighten the text – one of the tenets adopted by the Florentine *Camerata* in their concern for expression. What distinguishes the aims of the Florentine experimenters from those of Borromeo is that whereas they sought a dramatic and lyric expression that would move the emotions of the listeners, he demanded merely a clear presentation of the liturgical formula as a mode of religious edification. His demands were focused on the Mass – hardly a text to call forth emotional underscoring. He was against the profane, against spectacle (he forbade secular plays on religious holidays), and against the use of instruments in church music (though their use became ever more widespread, especially for sumptuous feastday ceremonial).[10] This ascetic, almost dogmatic side of Borromeo contrasted oddly with that revealed in his instructions on church building. Here all was to be directed towards impressing, overwhelming, and uplifting the faithful, and providing an environment as different as possible from their everyday one.[11] This outlook exudes the positive spirit of the Counter-Reformation, as his narrow attitude to music does not.

For the spirit of the Counter-Reformation was a positive one. Late sixteenth-century Catholicism showed itself in many ways not a historical changeling but a legitimate product of its historical age, reflecting in its own modes of praying and behaving and organizing, more perhaps than in its philosophizing, the general forces at work in contemporary society. Despite its limitations, the Counter-Reformation ensured the survival into the post-medieval world of a still-persuasive, still-expanding form of universal Christianity.[12] Along with a revival of the sacramental life of the Church, and the spread of new techniques of meditative prayer and eucharistic devotions, came a driving urge towards outward activity and good works as a factor in personal sanctification.[13] The asceticism of Borromeo was just one aspect of this tide. The genius of spirituality could take individual rather than corporate or liturgical expression, and this new individualism showed that Counter-Reformation religion was capable of assimilating humanistic elements.

Even if the Council of Trent's stipulations regarding music were limited, its general encouragement of clarity, simplicity, and an element of realism and even emotionalism in church art was undoubtedly fostered by the new climate of fervent spirituality and by the new outward-looking concern for the devotional well-being of the faithful at large. In church music itself this was reflected most of all in the way that composers depicted more graphically the spiritual moods of the texts they set in motets. This has nothing to do with word painting or madrigalisms in church music. It is illustrated best, perhaps, when the spiritual mood of the text coincides with the personal feelings of the composer, as in the case of Lassus in his later music; the dramatic and portentous mood of the motet *Scio enim* and the poignancy of the *Lagrime di San Pietro* provide examples of this. Palestrina, more emotionally detached, though affected by the trend towards clarity and simplicity in church music, was less disposed to respond so readily to contrasting spiritual atmospheres; a fervour typical of the Counter-Reformation does, however, inspire his *Song of Songs* settings of 1584.[14] Here is the sensuousness in church art mentioned earlier, found in music to Latin words but much akin to the vernacular spiritual madrigal – madrigalian, it is true, but not inspired by any secular ethic. Rome witnessed an even greater fervour and expressiveness in the Holy Week music of Victoria, even though this composer wrote no madrigals. But Victoria was a Spaniard, and it was Spain that produced St. Ignatius, the founder of one of the most important reform movements of the Counter-Reformation.

Jesuits and Oratorians

The importance of the Jesuits' role is expressed by Evennett when he writes:

Of this active, virile, exacting religious outlook of Counter-Reformation Catholicism . . . the Jesuits were the outstanding representatives. It was because they were so fully representative of all its main characteristics . . . that they became the outstanding force in the whole Counter-Reformation movement. . . . its modernisers . . . that [they] succeeded in impressing so much of [their] principles, outlook, and ethos on so many sides and parts of Catholic life and organization.[15]

The Society of Jesus set out to foster a personal spirituality in its members. Community prayers and long liturgical functions were reduced to a minimum. The Original Constitutions of the Order, laid down in 1540 by its founder St. Ignatius, forbade the recitation of the Divine Office in choir. Mortification of the body was discouraged. The cleansing of the soul by means of 'spiritual exercises', a novel idea, was not to take place in cloistered seclusion, without reference to the outside world; it was intended to prepare a man for active work as a soldier of the Church Militant. The Society of Jesus was monarchical and aristocratic, military in discipline and militant in missionary zeal, but it was utterly unmonastic, something new and appropriate to the post-medieval Church.[16]

Unmonastic, in that it was designed to serve ordinary people. Though opposed to scientific discourse, it was concerned with matters of the intellect and above all with education, not only of its own members but also of large numbers of the less privileged. St. Ignatius was against rigidity and insisted that his schools adapt to new ideas.[17] Gradenwitz, though writing about the eighteenth century, admirably expounds Jesuit aims in education that were equally valid in the early years of the order:

The Fathers who in Bohemia, Austria, Italy and South Germany supervised the nobility, the courts and education in general acted upon the principles prescribed in Rome for the order as a whole. The chief idea of the Jesuitic educational aim was that man should exploit all his worldly human faculties in order to attain to the utmost devotion, to a godly life and conduct, and to blessedness in the next world. In other words, to reach that world, the Jesuit employs every means at his disposal in this. Pomp and magnificence, ecstasy and sensuousness, all contribute their share to man's preparation for a spiritual life, and all this is effectively supported by art and music. In Jesuit drama it may be seen how the eternal conflict of mankind (sensuality against spirituality, ecstasy against contemplation) takes artistic shape, for side by side with the realistic action of the drama, which is represented with the most extravagant display, runs an allegorical action that invites meditation. Thus, in the theatre as in life, we find a parallel arrangement of contrasts.[18]

Such art is essentially outward-looking, showing concern for audience reaction, and it is precisely these features that underlie much early seventeenth-century church music, even more than that of the late sixteenth century. The concern to impress the spectator or listener echoes Borromeo's ideas on church building; the Jesuits would surely have approved in principle of the magnificence of large polychoral motets as a means of spiritually involving the faithful, since they applauded mighty architecture, sumptuous vestments, and altars of gold and silver.

, As for specific Jesuit attitudes to music, a recent study by Thomas Culley indicates its importance in the life of the German College in Rome, a seminary which was to prove a model for so many others erected throughout western Christendom by decree of the Council of Trent.[19] Typically for a Jesuit institution, the college admitted not only Germans training for clerical life but also young men from all over Europe, desirous of education, called *convittori*, whose number far exceeded that of the seminarians. The musical talents of the *convittori* were exploited early on, particularly in the 'Marian congregations', at which 'the *Salve Regina* is sung every night . . . with voices and instruments'. Such congregations (in effect devotional societies or sodalities) were a feature of Jesuit schooling, and embraced not only liturgical music but also vernacular songs and music for spiritual plays – music was associated with the Jesuit theatre from the beginning.[20]

Michael Lauretano, rector of the college from 1573 to 1587, was responsible for a considerable emphasis on liturgical decorum, and we can witness a characteristic Counter-Reformation concern for the tastes of the congregation in the following report of a decision of 1575:

But [Gregorian chant] is not tempered with such sweetness that it could be hoped that worldly men, or not too devout ecclesiastics, might, after some time, be kept [coming to the church] with that frequency with which they had begun. Lauretano, therefore, decided that instrumental music, and measured [music], the use of which had been accepted in the Church, were to be employed.[21]

It is clear that by this date the college 'had become a centre of liturgical music second to none in Rome; and S. Apollinare [its church] was one of the most frequented churches in the city'.[22] The *maestro di cappella* at this time was none other than Victoria. The relevance of this state of affairs at a Jesuit college to the development of church music in a wider context is aptly expressed by Max Wittwer:

The Council of Trent [decided] to found seminaries for priests patterned after the already existing Germanicum; and the measures taken in this institution for the musical formation of the clerics were to serve as an example. It is exclusively the merit of the Jesuits to have contributed to the elevation of church music in this area, since the clergy coming from the seminaries acquired not only a technical knowledge of music, but a knowledge of the literature as well, which they could, in their later spheres of activity, usefully employ.[23]

In contrast to the Jesuits, the Oratorians were laymen who met for informal prayer; despite their constitution and rule-book, they had a warm, almost modishly democratic, spirit. Their leader, St. Philip Neri, was a friend of St. Ignatius, and his spiritual exercises are a tame version of the original strict Jesuit ones. Their insistence on the text, the word, was a natural consequence of the Oratorians' fondness for biblical study; the beginnings of the oratorio as a musical genre stem from a fusion between this and the Jesuit moral theatre. Their musical requirements were of the humblest – simple vernacular *laude spirituali* in the first years of their existence – and we can see that the general modesty of means and the prayerfulness of many early seventeenth-century Italian motets while not conceived for their specific purposes, represent a continuation of Oratorian influence that coexisted with 'Jesuit' urges towards pomp and magnificence in grander music.

By 1600, the post-Tridentine style of Palestrina and others had served its purpose; it had satisfied the Council fathers as the first expression of the *novum genus* for which they had hoped. The time soon came when musical commentators would call it antiquated, even, in G. B. Doni's words, barbaric.[24] The new generation of composers, whose work is the subject of this study, envisaged the fulfilment of the Council of Trent's demands in monody and concertato, the styles of the day. Thus the styles of sacred and profane music came closer together, and some old-fashioned churchmen could find only profanity in anything that did not conform to the manner of Palestrina. One northern European Jesuit fulminated against the concertato idiom in these terms:

Without offence let me say, <u>ye musicians, that now a new species of singing is</u> dominant in the temples, but it <u>is showy, curtailed, dance-like, very little religious, indeed, but more suitable for theatre or dance than for the temple</u>. We seek artifice, and lose the pristine desire for prayer and chant. . . . What is this novel and tripping scheme of singing except a comedy, in which the singers are as it were the actors, with now one, now two, coming forward, and now the whole company, and conversing with modulated voices; presently one is again triumphant, but will soon follow the others. . . . This new-fangled way of singing, like some remarkable trick, introduces comedy into sacred edifices. . . . There were outstanding musicians in an early age, but truly, as even you will yourselves testify, those men sang differently and (if I may say so) more religiously. Their books of music your fastidiousness has long ago buried. <u>I beg you, let at least something of the old religiosity of sacred music be revived</u>. . . . <u>Let the music of the temples be of the kind which does not confuse prayer but arouses and kindles it.</u> [25]

<u>Such a protest was very probably directed at the all-pervading Italianate influence sweeping northwards across Europe in the early seventeenth century</u>, which affected sacred music as much as any other. There is no evidence that the Church officially frowned on the new styles of the day or attempted to pressurize her musicians into writing 'conservative' music, and every reason to suppose that the Counter-Reformation spirit, with all its positive manifestations, remained alive during the early years of the seventeenth century and favoured the development of Italian church music as much as did any extraneous transformations in musical style.

CHAPTER II

The Social and Geographical Context

ALTHOUGH, from the point of view of musical patronage, the transition from Renaissance to Baroque was that from an era in which church appointments held the greatest prestige to one in which composers of church music tended increasingly to hold court positions, this change was slow to take place in early seventeenth-century Italy, which boasted a distinctive race of church composers who had no connections with any court. The relative political stability of the last years of the sixteenth century may have allowed a number of courts – Ferrara, Mantua, Parma, Turin, and Florence – to flourish anew and become the leading cultural and social centres in the north of Italy, assuring their musical directors a fame at least equal to that enjoyed by those who held posts at St. Mark's, Venice or St. Peter's, Rome; but the most active and admired church composers, though they might have considered court positions attractive, often shone in more modest circumstances. It is even arguable that Monteverdi, one of the very few who had experience in both kinds of employment, produced his best sacred music while in a church post, even if he found the duties tedious and hankered after the freedom to continue composing for the stage.

The frenetic activity of the Venetian music publishers in the first half of the seventeenth century shows just how flourishing the church music industry was. A city's reputation could be upheld by its church music. That this was sociologically more significant than any other genre of art music is shown by the fact that, in an age before concert halls or even opera houses existed, with only a nascent middle class, the local church was the only place where music could be heard by the ordinary people – the citizens.[1] The aim of this chapter is to provide an overall view of the circumstances in which church composers worked, whether in the context of different kinds of post, or of the various cities and towns in northern Italy; a view which will prove complementary to plain biographical summaries of the lives of individual composers, and will demonstrate how talented musicians moved around in the course of their careers, bringing prestige now to one locality, now to another.

The bodies responsible for church music

We can divide the institutions that employed church composers in the early seventeenth century into three groups: the first consists of churches of cathedral status and a few ducal chapels; the second of ordinary provincial or local parish churches; and the third of charitable confraternities. In the geographical area of the Po basin (better called the *pianura padana*) and a few outlying districts there were at least seventy-three institutions employing a church composer as choirmaster; something under half of these fall into the first category of ducal chapels and churches of cathedral status.

These were the reasonably wealthy institutions, administered either by a council of lay people, as in the case of the most prestigious of all, St. Mark's, Venice, or by secular clergy, as with the lesser provincial cathedrals. In Venice, which was innately anti-clerical, church ceremonies were more tied to civic ritual than anywhere else, but in many other cities there was an element of integration between church and community. This is illustrated by the concern for the people's convenience shown by a church council decision at Bergamo in 1628, which delayed Vespers forty-five minutes so that the townsfolk could finish their evening meal in time to attend. Few cities had a court life – only Mantua and Parma among the large ones – and a big religious celebration was often a focal point in the calendar for both nobility and townspeople. At Venice the sacred festival of the Ascension and the civic expression of the Venetians' independence from the rest of Italy were combined in the famous ritual of 'the marriage to the sea', at which sumptuous church music overflowed from the basilica into *al fresco* performances. Even though such occasions involved more of the populace of a locality than similar ones which took place at a court, the courts are included with the prime category of appointment, since they not only had in their employ one of the greatest composers of the period – Monteverdi at Mantua – but also had the money to pay for elaborate music in their chapels as much as in their salons. If there are doubtful members of this category, they are the cathedrals of some very small country towns like Carpi or Este, which never managed to attract really gifted composers. On the other hand, some churches, though not called cathedrals, belong in this group for the same reasons as the courts.

②Most of the remaining appointments fall into the second category; ordinary parish churches in Venice or the provincial cities, and towns with just one church employing a composer. Although money might be less plentiful, or indeed severely limited at times, these appointments could attract some of the best church composers, since the conditions demanded a new small-scale, practical music for liturgical use, in which they could display their progressive tendencies. With this group belong one or two positions in convents and seminaries.

③ The third type of institution, the charitable confraternity, shared many characteristics of the provincial church. Organized by a body of altruistic lay people, it ministered to the poor and needy as well as running a small church with services and a choir. Again, although money was not usually plentiful with these bodies, small-scale music for their use was often supplied by very competent composers, who were surprisingly content with the modest emoluments paid out of members' monthly contributions. They went by different names in different cities; sometimes called *accademie*, they are not to be confused with the intellectual *accademie* that proliferated at the time, whose main concerns were literary and cultural. The most impressive charitable confraternities of the period were the six *scuole grandi* at Venice. These were wealthy and influential organizations, where solemn ceremonies became an occasion for splendour, delighting the participants. They commissioned works of art from painters and sculptors (for example, the fine series of paintings by Tintoretto still surviving at the Scuola di S. Rocco) and often enlisted the assistance of eminent musicians from St. Mark's.[2] Outside Venice, and less musically noteworthy, were two confraternities at Ferrara and one at Parma.

For all these institutions, whether great or small, the celebration of their patron saint's feast-day was the most solemn event in the calendar. In Venice, of course, ceremonial occasions were much more frequent, but in most cities and towns the main effort was directed at one particular feast in the church year. The limitations of a church's choir would be of no account; musicians from other churches in the city, or perhaps from neighbouring cities, would be hired to augment it in such a way that the most spectacular polychoral or orchestrally-accompanied church music could be performed. A procession through the streets would serve to integrate religious and secular festivities, and the town trumpeters might make an appearance.

This activity still bears witness to the ideals of the Counter-Reformation. In the first place, the concern of the church authorities with ordinary people and their civic pride on big occasions was a reflection of the outward-looking attitude recently adopted by the Church as a whole. Secondly, the charitable bodies, consisting as they did of lay people, were in some ways akin to St. Philip Neri's Oratorians; the distinction was that they were devoted to the service of the poor and needy rather than to private prayer. The kind of music used regularly in their chapels was spiritually similar in concept to the simple *laude* of the Oratorians – it was modest in means, affording no pretext for splendid sonorities or florid writing.

We may at this point examine the normal musical establishment at a typical large parish church in the provinces of northern Italy, which is as representative as any of the generality of church patronage in the early years of the seventeenth century – S. Maria Maggiore at Bergamo.[3] Set in a thriving city, this was a church with strong musical traditions built up in the late Renaissance, and with a succession of interesting names among its musicians in the Baroque period. It was run by a body called the Misericordia Maggiore, whose council of pious lay people had the composite aims of conducting the services of Mass and the Divine Office in S. Maria, maintaining its choir, running a school, and giving alms to the poor (as its name suggests); thus the organization represented a synthesis between the city church run solely by clerics and the confraternity run by lay people. Its income from wealthy patrons, amounting to some 20,000 *scudi* a year, raises it into our category of churches with cathedral status, though three-quarters of this sum was spent on the poor.[4] There were, in addition to the choir, resident priests who provided chant for the Hours of the Divine Office not sung chorally, and the plainsong portions of all choral observances. Choral music was required on most Sundays and some twenty-nine weekday feasts, at Mass and both first and second Vespers; though not all of it would have been elaborate (*falso bordone* chanting was popular for the psalms on less important days), the choir had a considerable amount to prepare.

Just as S. Maria Maggiore would augment its choir from outside for its greatest celebration (the feast of the Assumption), its own musicians were frequently invited to sing elsewhere when they were free, for a cathedral and several parish churches in the area had patron saints whose feastdays had to be dignified with solemn celebration. For some, singing by a cohort of the S. Maria choir was the only choral music they enjoyed; and there were rulings that the *maestro* himself, rather than a chorister, should direct these groups and earn a little extra above his salary. The *maestro*, usually assisted by the two organists, was also required to teach music at the attached school as part of his contract; this instruction included plainsong, measured music, and instrumental tuition on the organ, cornett, or trombone. Singing was also taught to the resident priests. The soprano singers would normally be recruited from the school, the other singers and players from outside. Such was the choir's fame that musicians often wrote to the church council offering their services, while the council, when it had vacancies, would consider singers recommended by choristers, and pay travelling expenses to those who came for audition, or even to an emissary who would scout around for talent. In addition to salaries, the musicians at S. Maria could receive payments in kind – quantities of grain and wine – as in the case of the *maestro* Giovanni Battista Crivelli, who in 1642 was given a large amount of grain and 300 litres of wine on account of his prodigious efforts organizing opulent music for Assumption Day by securing performers from all over northern Italy.

The size and composition of the regular choir varied considerably during the early seventeenth century, as shown by the figures for a number of individual years between 1614 and 1643:[5]

Year	Organists	S	A	T	B	Strings	Wind	Total
1614	2	4	1	1	2	2	3	15
1616	2	3	3	4	2	2	5	21
1618	2	1	1	1	1	—	—	6
1620	2	2	2	3	2	2	2	15
1628	2	6	3	5	2	1	2	21
1632	1	2	1	3	2	2	—	11
1643	1	1	2	1	1	3	—	9

The indications are that in 1616 the choir was rather large. Its size was more characteristic of the late Renaissance, and its repertory was drawn almost entirely from that era, with special emphasis on double-choir works (the persistence of two organists on the payroll is noteworthy). The choir at Bergamo can be contrasted with that of Modena Cathedral in 1615, which had about 15 singers, cornett, trombone, and organist. The drastically reduced total for 1618 represents first the aftermath of a period of inflation, which forced the church council to limit the total number of musicians to a maximum of sixteen, and then the effect upon the city of war, which for a few months brought all music at the church to a halt. Nevertheless, this emaciated body was hardly smaller than those in many other north Italian cities, and it forced the church, against its conservative inclinations, to consider modern small-scale music. We can see that, ten years later, the choir had regained its former size, but by then it was under a very famous 'modern' composer – Alessandro Grandi. After the disastrous plague of 1630 there was a predictably abrupt fall, and in the 1640s the small number of singers with the support of one organ and strings (not wind) was quite characteristic of a new epoch. The size of the choir over the years may be related both to external factors and to changes in musical taste, even if its response to these was somewhat delayed.[6]

The cities and towns where church music flourished

There were no fewer than nine cities in northern Italy with more than one church appointment occupied at some time by a church composer, who could become known by disseminating his music through publication. Venice, though it was undoubtedly the commercial hub of northern Italy and the principal centre of the music printing trade, must not be seen as the arbiter of church styles but as one fixed point amid the general stylistic diversity. Its domination of a large part of northern Italy was political rather than musical. As the map in the Appendix shows, the Republic of Venice stretched out in a line from east to west along the edge of the *pianura padana* which linked many fine cities – Treviso, Padua, Vicenza, Verona, Brescia, and Bergamo. Venice was famous as a libertarian stronghold. *Laissez-faire* in the conduct of life permeated all levels of Venetian society; *Siamo a Venezia* signified 'we are in a place of liberty!'. Provided that people did not meddle with political affairs, they were free to seek with impunity whatever pleasures appealed to them; Venice was a refuge for those who had suffered from intolerance elsewhere. She loathed the Pope, defied the papal interdict of 1606, and barred the clergy from any say in matters of criminal law. She welcomed Protestant students from the North, providing the opportunity for the young Schütz to witness Italian music at first hand under the tutelage of Giovanni Gabrieli. Nevertheless, this free-and-easy façade concealed the

Republic's political and economic decline. There was a passion for distractions and amusements which favoured music rather than art and sculpture[7] – music that might be anything from that included in vulgar comedies and buffooneries to the loftiest sacred motets. It is necessary to stress this atmosphere of cultural freedom, which in Venice and throughout the Republic seemed to encourage new trends in church music that were conspicuously absent from the music composed in cities, such as Milan and Bologna, under more reactionary powers.

There were, of course, a large number of church posts in Venice. St. Mark's had the positions of *maestro*, occupied by Monteverdi from 1613 to 1643, and vice-*maestro*, also often filled by composers of some reputation (Grandi, Rovetta) and potentially a stepping-stone to the top job, as it was for Rovetta, who succeeded Monteverdi on the latter's death. Then there were a number of local churches, often attached to monasteries. One of the most respected *maestri* at the Franciscan church of the Frari was the priest Giacomo Finetti from Ancona, who held the post from 1613 till his death from the plague in 1631. The Dominican church of SS. Giovanni e Paolo had music on a limited scale, directed by a series of organists which included Cavalli (1620–30) and Carlo Fillago (1631–44), the latter of whom was concurrently organist at St. Mark's. The Augustinian monk Carlo Milanuzzi was for a time organist in that order's church of S. Stefano, while there were other church composers active at S. Elena and the Madonna dell'Orto; it may well be that, since all these were organists and not *maestri*, music other than chant could only be heard on a limited number of occasions, as at SS. Giovanni e Paolo, or flourished for a limited period. Two of the Venetian confraternities were musically important; the Scuola di S. Giovanni Evangelista and the Scuola di S. Rocco. At the former, Francesco Usper and his nephew Gabriele, were employed at various times; the latter was the venue for the elaborate ceremonial music in honour of S. Rocco held in 1608 and later described by an English traveller, Thomas Coryat, in his *Crudities*. Giovanni Gabrieli, who provided and played chamber organs on this occasion, was the regular organist for this institution as well as at St. Mark's – another example of pluralism in Venetian musical employment – but his duties at S. Rocco were limited: to play at Mass on the first Sunday of every month and on a number of feast days, particularly Marian ones.[8]

The Veneto (the Venetian hinterland and the area to the north-east of Venice) was an important region for church music in the early seventeenth century. Small places like Murano (one of the Venetian islands), Chioggia, Asolo, Belluno, Noventa di Piave, and Portogruaro had some quite talented composers running the music in their parish churches. Chioggia was the birthplace of Giovanni Croce, *maestro* at St. Mark's from 1603 to 1609, while the organist at the church of S. Michele on Murano was the much travelled Orazio Tarditi. The other towns were relative backwaters[9] but the Veneto also had larger cathedral cities like Treviso, Udine, and Cividale del Friuli, about whose church music more is known.[10]

The most distinguished figure at Treviso cathedral in the early seventeenth century was Amadio Freddi, a Paduan by birth and pupil of Asola, that prolific north Italian church composer of the 1570s and '80s. He directed music there from 1615 to 1626, and his Mass and psalm collection of 1616 was one of the first collections by a provincial composer to include obbligato instrumental participation (for cornett and violin). The cathedral musicians often performed elsewhere, at the convent of S. Teonisto: on 9 June 1624 they were joined there by *maestri* and singers from Venice, and no less a figure than Giovanni Francesco Anerio from Rome, to celebrate the reception of novices. Freddi's connections were thus widespread – and he also contributed to the solo motet anthology *Ghirlanda sacra*. Carlo Fillago was organist at Treviso from 1608 till 1623, when he won the competition to become first organist at St. Mark's. An organ pupil of the Ferrarese madrigalist Luzzaschi, this talented player did not always enjoy good relations with Freddi, and was given to playing virtuoso pieces without the latter's permission. The church council resolved the dispute by stating that Freddi was 'the true head of the music', and that as such he would have to approve the organ music. In 1630, after Freddi's departure to Vicenza, the choir was about fourteen strong, but had no regular instrumentalists; in 1633, however, its activities were suspended through lack of funds.

For many years from before 1609, the music at Udine cathedral was in the hands of Monteverdi's somewhat mediocre predecessor at St. Mark's, Giulio Cesare Martinengo. He was followed by the Sienese Orindio Bartolini, who presided for the next twenty-six years, and founded a song school at which singing was taught three days a week, presumably to attract boy singers from the city itself. The local talent was probably inadequate, however, for in 1617 Bartolini had to go to Venice to seek new recruits. It is noteworthy that two of his three sacred publications appeared in the early 1630s, at a time when music publishing was at an almost complete standstill after the Venetian plague of 1630. The fact that all three were of large-scale music suggests that Udine may have retained a fairly big choir at least up to 1630. Its prestige was in no way diminished by his successor from 1635 to 1637, a young Venetian named Giovanni Antonio Rigatti who, though still in his early twenties, was already considered one of the finest musicians of the Veneto. Thanks to this reputation, his salary was half as much again as Bartolini's. Rigatti did not stay long, returning to Venice to take holy orders and teach singing at two of the Venetian *ospedali* (the *Mendicanti* and the *Incurabili*). He published no fewer than eight collections of church music between 1640 and his untimely death in 1648.

We may now consider the principal cities in the central geographical area of the Venetian Republic. First, and nearest to Venice, Padua, an important centre of music-making with a cathedral and the Basilica of S. Antonio, known often as the *Basilica del Santo*, or just *Il Santo*. Giulio Belli, who had worked at the Frari in Venice, was *maestro* there between 1606 and 1608 (but the style of his music belongs to the late sixteenth century). A stylistically more transitional figure is Giovanni Ghizzolo, who held the post in 1622–3; while Leandro Gallerano, *maestro* from 1624 to 1632, adopted a modern approach in using obbligato instruments in a hymn setting in honour of St. Anthony – two violins and trombone. During Belli's time the size of the choir was fixed at sixteen (four to a part), with the proviso that if the sopranos were too few a cornett would support their part; there were also five 'supernumeraries' – four trombones and one violin – who probably played only on certain solemn occasions, and whose main livelihood came from other engagements in churches, and perhaps in the town.[11] Both Ghizzolo and Gallerano wrote secular monodies, but from 1605 to 1614 Padua had been the home of a more important monodist, Bartolomeo Barbarino, who was a musician to the Bishop of Padua and who contributed to the early literature of sacred monody in his two motet books of 1610 and 1614. Freddi succeeded Gallerano as *maestro* at S. Antonio in 1632, and then held the same post at Padua Cathedral from 1634 to 1643;[12] between 1626 (when he left Treviso) and 1632 he had directed music at the cathedral of the next city westwards from Padua, Vicenza.

  Further west again was Verona, the doyen of whose church composers was Stefano Bernardi. Having spent a period at a parish church in Rome, he became *maestro* at Verona Cathedral in 1611 and remained there for eleven years. (His immediate predecessor was G. F. Anerio, one of the few Roman composers to hold a post in the north.) In 1616 Bernardi was associated with Verona's distinguished musical academy, the *Accademia Filarmonica*; some of his madrigals and ensemble music (the *Concerti accademici* of that year in particular) were intended for performances there. In 1641 Simone Zavaglioli held the post of cathedral *maestro*; the fact that both he and Bernardi published church music in both the 'old' and 'new' styles suggests perhaps a conservative orientation in the cathedral's music. We also have information about one of Verona's parish churches, S. Eufemia, where Carlo Milanuzzi was *maestro* in 1622. This composer was as widely travelled as any in Italy: though born in central Italy, he worked in Perugia, Verona, Venice, Modena, Camerino (near his birthplace), and the Piave area north of Venice. He was also a preacher and poet. Most of his appointments were modest; so was his music, which was mainly for a few voices and organ; he also found time to compose a number of secular monodies.

  Brescia, the next city westwards along the northern edge of the North Italian plain, was an important follower of Venetian trends. Although many of its churches had distinguished choirmasters and organists, it was not only the home of practical and theoretical musicians, but a veritable musical workshop, with its printers, organ-builders and lute-makers. Many of the organs that functioned regularly in concertato music all over northern Italy were built by the Antegnati family of Brescia. The city also had a violin-making school before Cremona, and could be considered as Venice's one serious rival in the field of the ensemble canzona;[13] its church composers Pietro Lappi, Cesario Gussago, and Francesco Turini all contributed to the genre, and Turini also to the early trio sonata. He was organist at the cathedral from 1620 onwards; but the church with which a greater number of composers were associated was S. Maria delle Gratie; Lappi directed its music from 1593 till his death in 1630, and its organists included Gussago and the very talented Giovanni Francesco Capello, whose church music was among the most boldly progressive of the decade 1610–20.[14]

The last of the larger cities of the Venetian Republic was Bergamo, close to the border with the Duchy of Milan. The principal church was S. Maria Maggiore, discussed earlier;[15] the adjacent cathedral had a much more modest musical establishment, and only one notable composer was associated with it – Tarquinio Merula, who simply moved 'across the way' some time after his abrupt dismissal from the post of *maestro* at S. Maria. This latter post was occupied from 1598 to 1626 by Giovanni Cavaccio, a comparative nonentity. As we have seen, the choir had its vicissitudes from time to time, but also enjoyed moments of achievement. With the aid of expense sheets showing payments to musicians hired *per diem* from outside,[16] we can build up a picture of the total array of performers assembled for Assumption Day 1621: a choir of sixteen (three sopranos, four altos, six tenors, and three basses), two violins, three viols, cornett, two trombones, and three organs (two being the fixed church organs, one an *organetto* brought in for the occasion). Polychoral and early concertato music with instrumental doubling would have been the order of the day, and the eight instrumentalists by themselves might have contributed canzonas. When Cavaccio's death opened a vacancy at S. Maria, Grandi, by then at the height of his career as Monteverdi's assistant at Venice, wrote to offer his services, and was invited to take up the post without interview or audition. He was no doubt anxious to have a choir of his own, especially in a place where modern music was not well known, and he built up the choir to a size where it could perform impressive music not only on big feasts but on a regular basis. He was also attracted to Bergamo, in part, by lower food prices, and though, when he revisited Venice, an attempt was made to lure him back, he stayed loyal to his new post. Assumption Day became an occasion of considerable splendour, and in 1628 Grandi invited singers from the Mantuan court, whom he probably came to know through Monteverdi. The plague of 1630 put a sudden end to this musical activity and, alas, claimed Grandi as a victim. Only five members of the choir survived; Grandi's successors were Merula and, after his dismissal, for 'behaving indecently with his pupils, to the grave scandal of this church', Cristoforo Guizzardo, an obscure figure whose health forced him to withdraw in 1636.

It was not until 1642 that the post was again filled by a composer of distinction, this time Giovanni Battista Crivelli, who had made many connections through his previous posts at Ferrara and Milan. Many of these former associates were invited – at vast expense – to partake in the Assumption Day celebrations of that year. The performers comprised a choir of twenty-one and an orchestra of five violins, viol, violone, and two bassoons, with three organs and *tiorba* as continuo. In later years. S. Maria gave employment to some important mid-baroque figures – Cazzati, Legrenzi, and Vitali.[17]

We now come to the four important cities of central northern Italy which were, or had been, flourishing court centres: Ferrara, Modena, Mantua, and Parma – places at which excellent music would be nothing out of the ordinary. Ferrara had ceased to be a court centre just before the beginning of our period: till 1598 it had been the residence of the Este family, under whose patronage some of the most influential secular music of the time had developed. When the Estensi transferred their residence to Modena in 1598, the courtly splendour came to an end, but the early years of the seventeenth century continued to produce solid achievements in the field of small-scale concertato church music. Ferrara's church posts included those at the cathedral and two charitable confraternities, all involving the performance of sacred music with limited resources but nevertheless able to attract some of the best talents of the age like Grandi, Donati, G. B. Crivelli, and, later, Cazzati. A large quantity of modest concertato motets were written by these composers when they were in the employ of one or other of the two confraternities, the *Accademia della Morte* and the *Accademia dello Spirito Santo*, especially the latter: Grandi produced three volumes between 1610 and 1614, Donati three in 1618 alone, and all had many reprintings. Clearly, the conditions at these establishments stimulated composers, and the results of their efforts achieved a wide popularity. That the groups of lay people that ran them held the provision of good music in high esteem can be seen from the fact that the 1636 regulation-book of the *Accademia dello Spirito Santo* devotes three out of eighteen chapters to musical matters. It is perhaps more than coincidence that this confraternity was founded in the very year that the Estensi ceded Ferrara to the papacy, with the possibile intention of evading the return of papal, and fully clerical, authority.[18] *Maestri* at the *Accademia della Morte* were sometimes the incumbents of the same post at the cathedral; in 1612, the *maestro*, Giovanni Ceresini, was also its chaplain and at the same time a beneficed priest of the cathedral. This suggests that the services were celebrated by priests provided by the latter institution, as Ferrara's main supply of secular clergy.

Modena, although in the sixteenth century a modest provincial town of secondary importance compared to Ferrara, was an interesting and typical centre of church music. With the arrival of the Este court there in 1598 it became a new cultural centre, exchanging roles with Ferrara.[19] A ducal choir was formed, directed from outside by the *maestro* of the cathedral. Modena Cathedral had acquired a good reputation for music under Orazio Vecchi, the celebrated madrigalist. Both he and his pupil Gemignano Capilupi wrote festive masque music for the Este court as well as music for the liturgy. Capilupi became consumed with rivalry for his teacher, and engineered his dismissal by reporting to the authorities that Vecchi had been conducting music in a nunnery, which was expressly forbidden. He was *maestro* from 1604 to 1614. The inventory of choir music consigned to him included works by Jachet of Mantua, Victoria, Morales, Palestrina, and Giacomo Fogliano (the last an early sixteenth-century *maestro* at the cathedral); the choir consisted of ten paid adult singers, a number of boy sopranos, and the organist. Later, in 1615, Giovanni Battista Stefanini took over the choir, to which a cornett and a trombone player were added. He was succeeded in 1626 by Paolo Bravusi, a pupil of Vecchi and formerly Capilupi's assistant, who saw works by both his predecessors through the press. His first appearance on the Modenese musical scene had been in 1608, when, at the age of twenty-two, he conducted an eight-part cornett and sackbut ensemble which processed in the city square to celebrate the arrival in Modena of Isabella of Savoy. Musical activity was drastically curtailed in 1630 by the deaths of Bravusi and many of the cathedral choir from the plague. In the ensuing decade the choir was transformed, because of financial difficulties typical of the time, into a group of solo singers and string players; the training of boys, and the use of polyphony requiring a full choir, could no longer be afforded.[20]

Mantua was a centre for court rather than church music, especially when Monteverdi was there. The post of *maestro* at the cathedral was quite a modest appointment, occupied at the turn of the seventeenth century by Viadana, a typical example of the unambitious, hard-working composer who was to be found in so many such posts. Monteverdi himself was not directly concerned with music at the ducal chapel of S. Barbara, and it appears that it was not this building but the large city church of S. Andrea that witnessed the exceptional brilliance of his Vespers music, published in 1610.[21] After this, there was nothing so bold in Mantuan church music until Cazzati's rich, colourful Mass and psalm settings written for the same church, and published in 1641.

Parma, the seat of the Farnese dukes, was another city with a lavish court life; it also had a cathedral and a confraternity (the *Compagnia della Steccata*). Giovanni Battista Chinelli, a native of the district, ran the music at the cathedral for two periods in the 1630s and '50s. Before his time, we learn of an Assumption Day celebration there in 1619 with music provided by twenty-one singers together with cornetts and trombones. At the confraternity, music was strictly organized, the rules of 1603 stating that choirmen would be fined if not in their places by the end of the Kyrie at Mass, or by the end of the first psalm at Vespers or Compline. This institution venerated the Virgin with particular solemnity, singing a regular Saturday Mass in her honour, and inviting musicians from the cathedral and ducal chapel to partake in special music on the feast of the Annunciation. The celebration of this occasion was proclaimed publicly by a fanfare of trumpets the previous day (in association with first Vespers, no doubt); on the day itself, these players performed canzonas and accompanied the singing of a procession at which the whole princely retinue of Parma was present.[22]

We now move from the Venetian Republic and the various duchies to areas under more repressive government – Bologna and Milan, at the two corners of the triangle marking the boundary of the *pianura padana*. Bologna was not only part of the Papal States, it had the oldest university in Europe and several monasteries which acted as conservative elements, and it had no court. Its cultural life was therefore rather austere, with musical life centred mainly on the churches and monastic chapels. Admittedly, its society was enlivened by that delightful Olivetan monk Adriano Banchieri, who amused the Bolognesi with his madrigal comedies and founded literary academies as well as writing informative treatises and unambitious church music. The post of choirmaster at the basilica of S. Petronio might be thought to be a very exalted one for a church musician, yet it did not come into its own until the mid-seventeenth century, when Cazzati began to raise the orchestral music there to a new and lasting level of fame. Earlier, the only prominent composer was Girolamo Giacobbi, and the organist's post was for many years held by a comparatively minor figure, Ottavio Vernizzi. Both these composers were involved with Bolognese *intermedi*, and both belonged to the *Accademia dei Filomusi* (Giacobbi founded this), which merged in 1624 with Banchieri's *Accademia dei Floridi*. The Oratorians established their first north Italian oratory in Bologna in 1615, but the city possessed no important charitable confraternities like those of nearby Ferrara.[23]

Milan and its environs were in rather different circumstances from those of Bologna and the Papal States: politically they were ruled by the reactionary Spaniards; ecclesiastically, Milan had been the centre of the north Italian Counter-Reformation under Carlo Borromeo, as we have seen. Although his strong censorship of things profane had prevented the influx of opera, dance and instrumental music did manage to gain a foothold. Strict adherence to the Tridentine stipulations and the lack of any wholesome influence from the new monodic styles caused many Milanese church composers to produce a rather dull, listless choral writing, but the city did become an important centre of the early church sonata, thanks particularly to the Cima brothers, Giovanni Paolo and Andrea. Certainly, its church music was thriving, there being in 1617 no fewer than seven churches with some kind of musical establishment. The resistance to secular influence resulted in the appearance in Milan of the best madrigals of the time – with sacred texts substituted for the originals; 'spiritual' editions of a selection of Monteverdi's were published by a Milanese editor, Aquilino Coppini. On the whole, the Counter-Reformation's effect at Milan was negative; the positive ideals of the Jesuits and Oratorians were hardly realized there. In the early years of the seventeenth century, its church composers were, on the whole, rather obscure organists, and it was some time before the city was able to boast of important names like Donati and Giovanni Battista Crivelli, who followed Vincenzo Pellegrini as *maestri* at the cathedral in the 1630s. It is interesting to note that the cathedral chapter used Monteverdi as a kind of consultant on musical matters, for example in 1625, when they sought his opinion on a potential successor to the mediocre Pellegrini. When Donati got the job in 1631 he may well have been recommended by Monteverdi.[24]

Of the smaller cities within the Spanish Duchy of Milan that were centres of church music, the most important was Novara, a short distance south-west of Milan and the westernmost city to concern us in this study. Despite wars and hardships, Novara had a cultural and intellectual life of its own in the sixteenth century – but this was a pale reflection of the splendours of court cities like Mantua and Ferrara. The proximity of Milan was partly to blame; the Spaniards, with their wars and lootings, had left seventeenth-century Novara in a sorry state. Even so, music at the cathedral kept going under a succession of interesting composers, including Giovanni Brunetti, Donati, Chinelli, and Gasparo Casati; the last was an important figure in Italian church music during the post-plague years, around 1640, but he died in his early thirties. The Mass music performed at the cathedral was contained in four large choirbooks, three devoted to Victoria and one to Morales; the presence of such music may have been the result of Spanish rule.[25] Certainly, it provides further evidence that for many years the best Renaissance polyphony was retained alongside newer music.[26]

Our survey of the main geographical area of northern Italy – Lombardy, the *pianura padana*, the Veneto, and the northern end of the Papal States – is now complete. Surprisingly, two other large centres figure hardly at all in the development of church music: Genoa and Turin. Andrea Bianchi worked at Genoa as well as Chiavari, also on the Ligurian coast. Early baroque musical activities at the Savoy court in Turin were concentrated upon theatre music; one of the very few church composers who served there was the Piedmontese Giovanni Battista Fergusio.

Certain other notable names have not been mentioned so far because they were only organists, not *maestri*, during the period: Serafino Patta and Michel' Angelo Grancini, both Milanese. Patta was a noted monodist, and travelled away from conservative Milan to Reggio Emilia and Cesena, while Grancini stayed put, distinguishing himself as Milan cathedral organist from 1630 to 1650, when he finally became *maestro*. Then again, there are a number of monastic composers who were not always full-time musicians, combining their musical activities with their priestly vocation. Giovanni Battista Biondi of Cesena and Arcangelo Borsaro of Reggio were especially prolific members of this group – Biondi had no less than fourteen publications of sacred music to his credit, and both had motets published in German anthologies. The category also includes two nuns, Caterina Assandra and Lucia Orsina (sometimes known as Vizzana).

Music in northern Italy was surprisingly unaffected by what was going on in Rome. Geographically and culturally, in fact, Venice was closer to that area north of the Alps which is now part of Austria than she was to Rome. Thus it is easy to understand why composers like Bernardi and Alessandro Gualtieri gravitated north to Salzburg, where the former was involved in the musical festivities for the consecration of the cathedral in 1628, composing a Te Deum and possibly a Mass for twelve choirs.[27] In the 1620s, Merula spent a period even further north, at the Polish court in Warsaw, and helped to maintain those ties between Poland and Italy which were also responsible for the remarkable collection of contemporary Italian sources now in the university library at Wrocław. Nearer home, the Habsburg court at Graz also attracted composers from northern Italy. As a result of its economic and cultural relations with Venice, Graz was the first Austrian centre of the cultivation of monody. The Counter-Reformation had had the effect of Italianizing the court; Prince Ferdinand refounded the choir in 1595, and before long musicians schooled in the Venetian style were being employed in the court chapel. The most distinguished of them was Giovanni Priuli, a pupil of Giovanni Gabrieli (who himself had played the organ for Ferdinand's wedding to Anna of Bavaria in 1600). When the court moved to Vienna in 1619, about four years after his appointment as *maestro*, Priuli continued to serve till 1622.[28]

In the foregoing pages some well-travelled composers with very active careers have come to light – Ignazio Donati, Carlo Milanuzzi, Orazio Tarditi, each with six or more successive appointments in widely separated locations – and many more unadventurous or unambitious musicians, a few of whom remained for many years in one post without lending it much glory or distinction. A typical career for a successful church composer was that of Grandi, who began at confraternities, graduated to a provincial cathedral, had a period as singer and vice-*maestro* with teaching duties at St. Mark's, and finally moved to a large and important provincial church (in his case, Bergamo). The prospects of promotion would have attracted him from Ferrara to Venice, but he left there after ten years because he did not, after all, see himself attaining the highest job in the foreseeable future (Monteverdi still had sixteen years of life ahead of him), and because the cost of living in Bergamo appeared less prohibitive for him and his numerous family. Any examination of how financial considerations influenced composers' decisions to move from job to job is complicated by the bewildering multiplicity of currencies.

Church music repertory and its dissemination

A number of references have been made to inventories as evidence of what choirs were performing or had available for performance; some of the choirs concerned turn out to be quite conservative. A characteristic example is again afforded by S. Maria Maggiore, Bergamo, where it was the custom for a list of the choir's repertory to be compiled with each change of *maestro*. The list compiled after Grandi's arrival in 1628 is the first in the seventeenth century, and it shows that the choice of music was indeed retrospective; there is strong emphasis on *cori spezzati* works by such composers as Asola, Croce, Viadana, Vecchi, and Giulio Belli, and also much from before the turn of the century.[29] Conspicuous is the almost complete absence of one-, two-, and three-part concertato motets, and except for a few contributions by Cavaccio in his last years as *maestro* (up to 1626) there seems to be no music less than ten years old. As we have seen, the choir had been quite large, possessing the right resources for performing the music of Morales, Lassus, Palestrina, and Victoria impossible for the normal 'modern' choir of far fewer voices. Some of its music had been in the repertory for over half a century. The situation began to change in the 1620s with the purchase in 1622 of several volumes of small-scale concertato music by Grandi, Leone Leoni, Leandro Gallerano, and others. In 1629, with Grandi as *maestro*, the most up-to-date music was being added – Grandi's own *Salmi brevi* and Carlo Milanuzzi's *Messe a3 concertate*, both issued in Venice that very year. In 1637 the choir obtained new motets by Giovanni Battista Crivelli, Galeazzo Sabbatini, and Francesco Colombini; by around 1650 the overall music list appeared better balanced between old and new, with far less polychoral music and more in the concertato idiom, some of it involving instruments.

Another view of the repertory can be gleaned from the stock catalogues dated 1619 and 1649 of one of the great Venetian music-publishing concerns, Vincenti.[30] In these the chief categories of motets, Masses, and Vespers collections are each divided into those with and without continuo. As we would expect, the proportion without continuo declines sharply between 1619 and 1649; for example, out of the twenty-seven sets without continuo in 1619, only fifteen remain in 1649, whereas sets with continuo increase from 117 in 1619 to 163 thirty years later. Composers of the former whose works stayed in stock include Palestrina (four books), Giovannelli, Rore, Andrea Gabrieli, and Asola; of the latter the composers are Aurelio Signoretti, Ercole Porta, Ignazio Donati, Grandi, Leone Leoni, Amadio Freddi, Carlo Milanuzzi, and others. And there are of course new names in the 1649 list: Tarquinio Merula, Giovanni Rovetta, Orazio Tarditi, Sigismondo d'India, and Giovanni Antonio Rigatti appear as composers of motets. For the organist, there are tablatures of music by the Gabrielis,

Padovano, Merulo, and Banchieri, and even harpsichord dances by the Venetian organist Giovanni Picchi. The supply of Compline collections, litanies, and Magnificats remains much the same in the two catalogues, many of their composers being represented in both; just as with Anglican service music today, in many churches fixed liturgies of this kind were sung to a number of standard settings.

Venice's music printing industry had been expanding steadily since the days of Petrucci. It was responsible, through the principal firms of Vincenti, Amadino, and Gardano, and his heir Magni, for the publication of perhaps nine-tenths of early seventeenth-century church music in northern Italy.[31] Composers' dedications were almost always dated and signed from there, and composers themselves must have come from near and far to sell their music to the publishers and purchase material for their choirs. The sheer volume of small-scale concertato music emanating from Venice's publishers is perhaps the best guide of all to the popularity of new music in the modern style, and assures us that old-fashioned repertoires like that of Bergamo were not necessarily the rule. Another testimony to the flourishing state of church music publication was the appearance of anthologies of various kinds.[32] In the sixteenth century, Venetian anthologies had been overwhelmingly devoted to the propagation of madrigals, for that period was the heyday of the genre. With the decline of the conventional five-part madrigal, it became the turn of new church music to benefit from this means of dissemination, by which the names of the great rubbed shoulders with those of many modest but talented figures in a truly representative fashion. Some of the anthologies represented groups of composers in a particular city or court, such as G. B. Bonometti's *Parnassus Musicus Ferdinandeus* (RISM 1615[13]), dedicated to Prince Ferdinand of Graz. It contained works by nine composers in the prince's service and by others whom the editor had encountered in his previous career at Bergamo and Milan (Priuli, Cavaccio, Andrea Cima, and Pellegrini among them). For others, like the four edited by Lorenzo Calvi (RISM 1620[2], 1624[2], 1626[3], and 1629[5]), the net was cast widely among the most able talents of the day. These particular collections contain a good deal of music not already available in volumes by individual composers – they are unique sources for eight works by Monteverdi and ten by Grandi. *Ghirlanda sacra* (RISM 1625[2]), compiled by Leonardo Simonetti, a singer at St. Mark's, was the first anthology of solo motets. It contains four pieces each by Monteverdi and Grandi, and other contributions from the best monodists of the day. Anthology compilers were often cathedral singers; Francesco Lucino, employed in this capacity at Milan, brought out two anthologies of Milanese concertato music (RISM 1608[13] and 1617[2]) with the Milanese printer Lomazzo, who himself edited a further volume (RISM 1626[5]). Milan had its own publishing concerns, though they were far less important than Venice's, and tended to be parochial in interest, dealing with music written in and around the city. In conclusion, we must recall that a certain amount of north Italian church music was published in German anthologies for both the Protestant and Catholic markets, edited by such men as Johann Donfrid and Ambrosius Profe; though much of this was reprinted from the existing Italian editions, its appearance north of the Alps reflects a historical cross-current of considerable significance.

CHAPTER III

⟡

The Liturgical Context

PUBLICATIONS of church music in northern Italy in the early seventeenth century tended to fall into three groups: those of motets (often called *concerti*); those of psalms (including the Magnificat); and those of Masses. The last two groups contained music destined for specific services, and indeed psalm collections might include one setting of the Mass – as is shown by the frequency of the title *Messa e salmi*. Motet collections, on the other hand, served all sorts of purposes both within and outside the context of church services; aspects of these will be discussed later. It is clear that the principal rites carried out in most churches were Mass and the Office of Vespers – a situation which in fact prevailed in many of the larger Catholic churches in Europe until recent liturgical changes. This fact is confirmed by the steady flow of Masses and Vesper psalm publications written by composers all over the provinces of northern Italy. The general practice at these services was to mix plainsong (often called *canto fermo*) with measured music (*canto figurato*) for those items that were sung, and to add organ and ensemble music by way of prelude, interlude, or postlude to the service, or indeed in place of various sung items. There was nothing incongruous about the intimate juxtaposition of plainsong, the age-old chant of the church, and up-to-date part-music; the performance of *alternatim* psalms, hymns, and Magnificats already had a respectable tradition going back a hundred years and more. Although many composers abandoned this practice when it involved a confrontation of unaccompanied plainsong with the accompanied concertato idiom, the idea of interspersing whole plainsong items with whole newly-composed ones was essential to the then-fashionable notion of a liturgical 'mix'.

What were the days in the liturgical calendar when some polyphonic music was normally sung? It is of course difficult to generalize, but some overall idea can be gleaned from the categories of feasts at which the use of the organ was approved, as indicated in Adriano Banchieri's *L'organo suonarino* (1605), a compendium of advice for organists in monastic and parochial positions. That this book was still popular enough to be reissued in 1638 is perhaps an indication of the widespread applicability of Banchieri's suggestions. He lists (1) feasts of the Virgin, (2) Sundays, (3) feasts of Our Lord, Saints, and Apostles, (4) Corpus Christi, (5) feasts of Angels, and the night of Christmas Eve, (6) Octaves – i.e. the week after a great feast, (7)

Easter and similar solemn feasts, and (8) feasts of Martyrs, Confessors, and church dedications. He reiterates the rule that the organ be silent in Lent and Advent except on 'Laetare' and 'Gaudete' Sundays, respectively the fourth in Lent and third in Advent. The list may serve as a guideline, since it covers most of the days on which there was likely to be measured music of some kind. It is not clear whether the order in which Banchieri places the categories represents a hierarchy of importance, but it would be quite characteristic of the emphasis in baroque liturgy that the Marian feasts come first on the list, whereas Easter, in reality the most solemn occasion of the Church year, is placed seventh.

In many places, specific feasts were accorded special importance. In Venice, these included the days when the Doge attended services in St. Mark's, when not only voices but also instruments were required.[1] In addition to feasts like Christmas, Easter and St. Mark's Day, they included such occasions of civic celebration as the anniversary of a Doge's coronation, as well as the famous *Bucintoro* or 'marriage to the sea' ceremony on the Vigil of Ascension Day – instances of the integrated church-state festivity peculiar to Venice.

A somewhat fuller amplification of Banchieri's list of major feasts is found in a church council minute of 1622 at S. Maria Maggiore, Bergamo, an establishment fairly representative of the provinces. This includes Palm Sunday, the last four days of Holy Week, Easter Sunday to Tuesday, Whit Sunday to Tuesday, Trinity Sunday; Christmas, Circumcision, Epiphany, Ascension, Corpus Christi; the Conception, Nativity, Annunciation, Visitation, Purification, and Assumption of the Virgin; the feasts of the Conversion of St. Paul, St. Mark, St. John before the Latin Gate, St. John the Baptist, SS. Peter and Paul, S. Rocco, St. Sebastian, All Saints, All Souls, St. Stephen, and St. John the Evangelist.[2] A note one year later tells us that Mass was to be sung in measured music on all these feasts and on all Sundays, except at harvest or carnival time and on the first five Sundays of Lent. The whole of Vespers was to be sung this way as well, except on ordinary Sundays, when only two or three psalms, the hymn, and Magnificat were to be sung in measured music, the rest to plainsong.[3]

The 1603 regulations of the *Compagnia della Steccata* at Parma give us some idea of the measured music requirements at a typical confraternity. Clearly, there was less emphasis on the Mass than on the Offices, for Mass was dignified by music only on the feasts of Christmas, St. Joseph, St. John the Baptist, the Coronation of the Virgin, and All Souls; whereas Vespers was to be sung in measured music throughout on some of these days and many others, including every day from Christmas Eve to the Epiphany (6 January) and three other feasts of Our Lord, three of the Virgin, four saints' days, and the dedication day of the chapel.[4] Vespers required two services per feast, first Vespers on its vigil and second Vespers on the day itself.

The Mass

Although it was common practice for large parts of the liturgical action of the Mass to be accompanied by various kinds of music, it is evident that there was concern lest the music should distract attention from the liturgy. Of the movements of the Ordinary of the Mass, the Kyrie, Gloria and Credo presented no difficulty in this regard, for they were sung in what was essentially an introductory part of the service; the ministers and congregation were with the choir in spirit, and free to be uplifted to heavenly thoughts by harmonious music. On the other hand, more extended settings of the Sanctus and Agnus Dei could appear to cover up and distract from the important liturgical preparation for the Consecration and Communion. Here it was felt that the accompanying music should be instrumental, or, if vocal, should consist of some motet directly connected with these moments of the Mass. Thus it was that settings of the Sanctus and Agnus Dei were shortened, by omitting some of the text, in order to grant a place to such items. For example, Banchieri's three-part Masses of 1620 have Sanctus settings that end with the first 'Hosanna' or even at 'Sabaoth', and Agnus Dei movements which consist of only one invocation ending 'miserere nobis'. The Mass that Ignazio Donati appends to his *Salmi boscarecci* of 1623 has a Sanctus and Agnus Dei which, he tells us, are 'set briefly according to the Venetian manner' so as to give way to a *concerto* for the Elevation, and a *sinfonia* at the Communion. The ultimate solution was not to set the Sanctus and Agnus Dei at all; this happened in many large-scale ceremonial Masses, where long settings of these movements would be in danger of holding up, if not engulfing, the liturgical action.[5] Where they were set, the music was brief, as in Ercole Porta's Mass of 1620.

Such extra-liturgical music was by no means limited to the Elevation and Communion of the Mass. Once again, Banchieri's *L'organo suonarino* makes several constructive suggestions to the organist. Among them are a forty-bar fugue to be played at the Gradual followed by a twelve-bar Alleluia, two very short flourishes at the Sanctus, solemn soft music at the Elevation to move the people to devotion, a light canzona after the Agnus Dei, and a short flourish after the final dismissal. He recommends that the repetition of the Introit Antiphon after its psalm verse be dispensed with, and that a motet be performed at the Offertory. Among a number of organ pieces printed at the back of the volume are a toccata for the Elevation and flourishes for the entry and exit of the priest before and after Mass. Now it is clear from these suggestions that Banchieri countenanced more than the insertion of organ interludes; some of these pieces were actually to be played during certain items of the Proper of the Mass while the priest said the relevant texts quietly at the altar. Such a practice was in line with the stipulations of the Church laid down in the *Caeremoniale* of 1606,[6] and constitutes one of several pieces of evidence that the items of the Proper were not necessarily performed to their correct texts by the choir; provided these were read by the priest, other vocal music ('Proper substitutes') could be sung simultaneously, or instrumental music played. The use of such substitutes was, indeed, part of a tradition going back at least a century.

Other evidence for the use of Proper substitutes comes from Banchieri's *Messa solenne* of 1599 and Carlo Milanuzzi's *Missa plenarium* of 1622. It is clear from the latter that at solemn celebrations when the choir was not singing a Proper substitute, organ or ensemble music was preferred to the chanting of plainsong, and that plainsong, even to the correct liturgical text, was not regarded as sufficiently festive.[7] A particularly interesting collection from the liturgical point of view is Amante Franzoni's *Apparato musicale* of 1613, which may well represent the practice at Mantua during Monteverdi's time there (it contains a work for soprano and four trombones based on a repeated litany invocation, in the manner of Monteverdi's *Sonata sopra Sancta Maria*). Franzoni provides the following music for the Mass:

> Entrata et Ritornelli a quattro per l'Introito
> Canzon Francese a quattro per l'Epistola (La Gonzaga)
> Laudemus Dominum et sue Sinfonie a otto per l'Offertorio
> Sinfonia al Sanctus a quattro
> Aperi oculos tuos a quattro per la Elevatione
> Sinfonia all'Agnus a quattro
> Canzon a quattro, due soprani, e due Bassi nel fine[8]

This scheme demonstrates a characteristic latitude of liturgical practice: three of the Proper items are suppressed in favour of other music (*per l'Epistola* most likely means *after* the Epistle, i.e. during the Gradual), and instrumental *sinfonie* are played at the Sanctus and Agnus Dei. Apart from practices like these described in individual publications, another pointer to the demise of choral performance of correct liturgical Propers early in the seventeenth century is to be seen in the changing nature of church music collections themselves. Whereas cycles of Introits or Offertories (e.g. those of Palestrina) frequently appeared in the late sixteenth century, none whatsoever were issued in Italy between 1611 (Introits by Valerio Bona) and 1742.[9]

Banchieri's suggestions for extra-liturgical organ music were aimed at modest establishments, but it is clear that in those places which possessed a resident church orchestra (above all, St. Mark's, Venice), ensemble music was increasingly prominent; collections of organ toccatas – including those quiet and mystical pieces written to be performed during the Elevation of the Host – give way to those of ensemble canzonas and violin sonatas.[10] At St. Mark's, the Gradual and the Elevation were the parts of the service especially emphasized by the use of instrumental music, the ensemble types being appropriate at the Gradual and solo pieces at the Elevation. Although, as we have seen, the orchestra was normally required only on the most important categories of feasts, there were six lesser occasions in the Church's year when it was expected to perform at the Gradual in otherwise *a cappella* (unaccompanied) Masses;[11] here its music would have provided a striking contrast to the old, less flamboyant style of the choral items. In this connection, it may be observed that Giovanni Gabrieli wrote scarcely any music for the Mass Ordinary; his splendid polychoral canzonas and sonatas would customarily have rubbed shoulders, on big occasions, with more restrained Mass settings.

A brief word may be said about Banchieri's methods, expounded again in *L'organo suonarino*, of singing the Mass in monasteries where choirs were extremely limited. Quite simply, he uses plainsong melodies as a basis for an *alternatim* setting, the chant alternating with a freely derived bass line in measured music, which is sung by the monks and harmonized as a figured bass by the organist. He expects the organist to treat occasional verses fugally by cueing in an imitative entry for the right hand. Here, then, is proof that the ancient chant of the Church was considered quite adaptable to the most rough-and-ready modern performance methods.

The Office of Vespers

Whereas the Mass was accompanied by a fair amount of extra non-liturgical music spaced out by liturgical action, the Office of Vespers allowed less room for it, since the items sung to music were performed in a more concentrated sequence. These included the opening responses, five psalms, each with its own antiphon, a hymn, the Magnificat and its antiphon, and (if Compline were not to follow) one of the four Marian antiphons at the end.[12] If the practice at S. Maria Maggiore, Bergamo, is any guide, then the greater part of Vespers, including two or three psalms out of five, was to be sung to measured music. Musical settings of the psalms were lengthy, and had nothing but through-composed works been used, the Office would have taken up some considerable time. However, measured music (*canto figurato*) at Bergamo clearly included the use of *falso bordone*, a method of harmonized chanting of the psalms, evolved in the late sixteenth century, which was almost as economical in terms of time as the plainsong psalm tones themselves. Not that there seems to have been any objection to long choral Vespers services, at least on great feasts; the sumptuous Vespers in Venice attended by the English traveller Thomas Coryat in 1608 took several hours,[13] and a complete performance of Monteverdi's grandiose 1610 Vespers is leisurely in pace.

The character of Vespers music publications was changing around the year 1600. Whereas, earlier in the Renaissance, musical settings of hymns and Magnificats were most common, there had since 1570 been something of an explosion in the publication of psalm settings, which incorporated both the simple choral style and the technique of *falso bordone* as a means of fulfilling Tridentine dictates about verbal intelligibility; the actual psalms set were intended to cover all the major feasts of the church year, and one or more Magnificats would be included. Around 1600, collections began to be more varied in content; instead of up to twenty psalms, only the most common ones required by the liturgical calendar (many of which occurred on several different categories of feasts) were provided, together with, perhaps, the responses, two Magnificats, *falsi bordoni* to all the tones, and some motets. Collections along these lines were much more adaptable, enabling a *maestro di cappella* to perform Vespers elaborately on a large number of occasions; certainly, adaptability to changing liturgical needs, as indeed to differing musical resources, became a typical feature of early baroque publications.[14] The decline of the homogeneous liturgical collection and the rise of the 'compendium' of diverse elements also sets the scene for more exceptional compilations like Monteverdi's 1610 Vespers. The increasing emphasis on Vespers music during the early seventeenth century is confirmed by the fact that in the stocklists of the Venetian publisher Vincenti, psalm collections multiply tenfold between 1591 and 1662, whereas those of Masses multiply only fivefold.[15] The items of Vespers music least consistently found in compilations were settings of hymns and Marian antiphons. In the case of hymns, sixteenth-century polyphonic settings survived long into the seventeenth century, and Pietro Lappi's hymns of 1628 were a comparative rarity; they are written in an archaic style, for *alternatim* performance. The Marian antiphons were most often found in Compline or motet collections rather than in Vespers compilations; they were probably used not only as conclusions to the Office, but also as motets suitable for Mass on Marian feasts, a tradition which goes well back into the previous century before the Office became adorned with so much measured music. If hymns and Marian antiphons were not usually included in Vespers publications, the Magnificat was ubiquitous, often with two settings. If these required forces distinctly different in size, it could be that the simpler one was sung at first Vespers on the evening previous to the feast, and the more elaborate one reserved for second Vespers on the feast-day itself;[16] or, perhaps more plausibly, it may be that the choice was made according to the musical resources of the choir. Psalm collections might often include not just two alternative Magnificats, but alternative choices of psalm settings too. Even such a special publication as Monteverdi's Vespers, which is suitable only for Marian feasts, contains alternative Magnificats, the larger requiring obbligato instrumental participation; one of the psalms, *Dixit Dominus*, has optional instrumental passages and is thus adaptable to different circumstances.[17] It is quite possible that, for some modest establishments where its performance as a complete entity was unthinkable, this collection provided a supply of individual settings to be worked through on the various Marian feasts of the year, as and when resources permitted.

On the other hand, there now seems little doubt that Monteverdi's Vespers could have been performed as an authentic liturgical sequence. The key to this formerly vexed issue lies in deciding what was the customary practice regarding those items of the Vespers liturgy that were proper to each feast – the psalm and Magnificat antiphons. These items varied in exactly the same way as the Proper of the Mass, and evidence from many different sources makes it clear that they received the same musical treatment as Mass Propers – that is to say, provided the texts were recited quietly by the officiating priest, other music to other texts could be performed by the choir. In the case of Vespers, there was an additional incentive to substitute freely chosen music; it was a way of circumventing the rule that a psalm or Magnificat should be in the same plainsong mode as its antiphon. If the choirmaster ignored the correct antiphon text, he need no longer be bound to use a psalm setting in the stipulated mode, and therefore had a much wider choice of psalm music too. It is in the light of this departure from the strict liturgical formula that the interpolation of motets in Monteverdi's Vespers can be seen to belong to a total scheme that was quite authentic.[18] It was, admittedly, very rare for motets to be interspersed with psalms in an actual publication. The *Salmi* of 1619 by the Roman Paolo Agostini is the only other one of the time known to be set out in this manner.[19] The same scheme is suggested in Giovanni Battista Fergusio's *Motetti e dialoghi* of 1612 by the groupings of seven pieces – six motets and one Magnificat – of which the motets could have served as antiphon substitutes to five psalms and the Magnificat.[20] Leandro Gallerano's *Messa e salmi* of 1629 is more explicit, prefacing the first psalm and the Magnificat setting with introductory motets. As in the case of Mass Propers, instrumental music might also be played during the recitation of the antiphons. Banchieri mentions this practice, which is confirmed by Giovanni Battista Fasolo's *Annuale* (1645); the latter indicates that for occasions of greater festivity an ensemble piece might be more appropriate than organ music.[21] Even a document as official as the *Caeremoniale* of 1670 sanctions organ music at the antiphons of Vespers. On the other hand, a papal decree issued by Alexander VII in 1657 forbade the use of non-liturgical texts in liturgical rites – sufficient proof of what the highest authorities would have regarded as an abuse. The fact that Monteverdi does not provide antiphon substitutes for the Magnificat in his Vespers may suggest that instrumental music would have been played at this point.[22]

Other Offices and rites

Apart from Vespers, the only other Office sung to any great extent in measured music was Compline. This, the final Office of the day, took place either before the evening meal or as the day's last act. The practice of setting Compline psalms to music arose at the same time as that of setting Vespers psalms – around 1570 – but its minor position can be judged by the fact that Compline music publications totalled at most only a quarter of the number of Vespers collections from this date right through into the seventeenth century. Only certain churches provided a choral Compline, and there was therefore a correspondingly small demand for published settings. Where it was sung, the service might occur in certain seasons of the Church year. For instance, at S. Maria Maggiore, Bergamo, Compline was sung only during the second half of Lent,[23] and in 1628 the choir's library possessed eight sets of Compline music compared with thirty-five of Vespers psalms. Compline was also regularly sung in Lent at the *Compagnia della Steccata* at Parma – daily from the first Saturday, to the Tuesday of Holy Week. Outside Lent, the members of the confraternity would sing Compline weekly, on Saturdays, with a litany at the end, and on certain big feasts and their vigils.[24] Outside monastic establishments, it was probably the confraternities rather than parish churches, who sang Compline, for the musical items varied little throughout the year (unlike those of Vespers) and would not have required a large repertory. They consisted of four fixed psalms (nos. 4, 30, 90, and 133 in the Vulgate numbering),[25] the hymn *Te lucis*, the short responsory *In manus tuas*, the Nunc dimittis, and the Marian antiphon appropriate to the season; this last item was normally performed at the end of Compline. Most publications of Compline music could thus be comprehensive without becoming voluminous. A typical example of the early years of the seventeenth century was Viadana's double-choir Compline of 1606, which provided *falso bordone* responses and very simple syllabic declamation in the psalms. Even though Compline had no proper antiphons to furnish a pretext for substitute motets or other music, Viadana was still concerned for musical variety, proposing that the organist add a *concerto* after Psalm 4, and a short interlude in the correct mode half-way through Psalm 90. By the late 1630s, Compline music was being written in the most progressive concertato idiom with obbligato violins, as we can see from Giovanni Battista Chinelli's publication of 1639 and Rigatti's of 1646. We may recall that Chinelli worked in Parma, home of the confraternity referred to above, which needed a fair amount of Compline music. As to the destination of Giovanni Antonio Rigatti's setting, we may guess that, since in the year of its appearance he described himself as choirmaster to the Patriarch of Venice, its elaborate music might have accompanied this prelate's private Compline service.[26]

A small number of liturgical publications of music which did not fit the categories of motets, Masses, and Vespers compilations were intended for more specific rites or Church seasons, defying the trend towards comprehensiveness and adaptability. To judge from the many masterly settings of the Requiem Mass written during the Renaissance that are well known to us, we might be surprised to find that very few were published in northern Italy in the early seventeenth century. Arcangelo Borsaro issued a set of Requiem music for double choir in 1608, and Orindio Bartolini's 1633 Masses included a Requiem which may have been written for special circumstances. It is likely that simple plainsong or older polyphonic settings were considered more fitting for obsequies, so that there was no demand for settings in the new style. Not that this style was regarded as necessarily incompatible with melancholy liturgical occasions; of the few collections of Holy Week music, including settings of the Lamentations, Benedictus, and Miserere for the special Office of Tenebrae, that by Giovanni Francesco Capello (1612) was in an up-to-date idiom with rich instrumental accompaniment. But again, by comparison with their heyday in the Renaissance, the Lamentations in particular were very seldom set in the early Baroque – only eleven sets were issued at Venice between 1600 and 1620.[27] Giovanni Bacilieri's Holy Week collection of 1607 was written in the traditional style, with *falso bordone* chanting for the Miserere, *alternatim* polyphony for the Benedictus, and *turba* choruses in the two Passion settings for Palm Sunday and Good Friday respectively. Such collections provided music for various different services; perhaps the most limited of all in function was a set of music for Christmas night (*Omnia in nocte Nativitatis Domini*), published in 1609 by Giacomo Finetti. It is worth noting that most of these specialized compilations appeared early in the century, and that many harked back to the Renaissance polyphonic style.

The choice of texts for motets

Although the term 'liturgical music' may normally be understood to embrace all church music written for performance in connection with the sacred rites – as distinct from works of a general religious tone such as cantatas and oratorios – it also has a more specialized meaning: actual settings of texts prescribed by the liturgical books for any particular day or feast. This meaning will be used in the following discussion of the choice composers made of texts for their motets, or *concerti* – the latter a contemporary term for anything that was not a Mass, a complete psalm setting, or some other strictly liturgical entity; therefore any text that does not correlate with those given in the liturgical books will be treated as 'extra-liturgical' in this stricter sense.

In considering texts let us examine the motet output of two composers, Viadana and Grandi, broadly representative of northern Italy in their selection. The extra-liturgical texts have been sorted out from the liturgical, which have in turn been grouped by type. In the case of Grandi, the 130 motets in his published collections for more than one voice and without obbligato instruments (seven volumes in all) were considered. Of these, sixty-four proved to be liturgical, and Table I shows how these are derived from the various rites according to the Roman Missal and Breviary.

Table I. *Sources of Grandi's liturgical texts*

Mass Propers	14
Office antiphons	17
BVM antiphons (Vespers/Compline)	3
Hymns	1
Matins responsories	21
Composite	8

It is probably significant that the liturgical pieces were written largely when Grandi was working as *maestro di cappella* at the *accademie* in Ferrara, and that the two books published after he had gone to Venice contained a larger proportion of extra-liturgical pieces. At Venice the emphasis was evidently upon Vespers music – psalms and hymns – as can be seen from lists of Monteverdi's published church music; the many extra-liturgical texts set after 1620 by Grandi and Monteverdi, especially those in Grandi's four books for solo voice with or without obbligato instruments (omitted in the preparation of Table I), were as likely to have been sung in aristocratic domestic circles as in church – a situation peculiar to a city like Venice. Even among the liturgical category in these books, the proportion of composite, freely-assembled texts increases sharply.[28] Table II is based upon the 158 motets in Viadana's *Cento concerti* of 1602 and the two subsequent supplementary volumes.[29]

Table II. *Liturgical functions of Viadana's texts*

Office	Proper of the Time	54
	Proper of the Saints	5
	Common of the Saints	8
	Ordinary	30
	General	4
Mass and Office	Proper of the Time	8
	Proper of the Saints	1
	Both	1
Mass	Proper of the Time	8
	Proper of the Saints	1
Extra-liturgical		38
Total		158

Here the distinction is made between the different liturgical cycles rather than between antiphons, responsories, hymns, and so forth.

About one fifth of the texts set by Grandi are Mass Propers, selected from a wide variety of feasts and ordinary Sundays in the Church year. But there is in no sense an attempt to provide a comprehensive collection for the whole year (as with compilations of Vesper psalms), nor are the motets ever marked as intended for any particular feast. The absence of any such systematic setting of Mass Propers suggests that these parts of the service were usually either sung to plainsong or, as described above, recited by the celebrant to the accompaniment of a Proper substitute from the choir. The random provision of motets whose texts were Mass Propers suggests that choirmasters were sometimes able, or willing, to perform their own or another composer's setting of a Proper antiphon from time to time. But such settings may equally never have been intended to be sung in their liturgically correct position at all. The text of Grandi's motet *Sicut oculi servorum* (psalm 122, verse 2), for instance, happens to be the Introit for the first Monday in Lent (the one season during which each weekday has its own Proper); but except in the highly improbable event of Mass being celebrated with music on a weekday, this motet could never have fulfilled its liturgical function as an Introit antiphon. It might possibly have been used as an Introit substitute on the previous Sunday, or as a motet for general use in Lent.

This leads on naturally to consideration of motets whose texts consist of randomly selected, isolated psalm verses. A fair number of Grandi's non-liturgical texts come under this heading and, by and large, such motets were of general as well as specific use, for the psalms were by no means associated with particular parts of the Church year, let alone individual feasts. Many of the stipulated Proper texts – such as *Cantate Domino* or *Jubilate Deo*, to name two very common motet texts – were themselves drawn from psalms, but it is more likely that composers elected to set them *qua* appropriate psalm verse than *qua* Mass Proper for one given Sunday. Though there is enough evidence for the practice of antiphon substitution, the whole question of whether motets whose texts coincide with Mass Propers were ever sung in their correct place or served as extra-liturgical interpolations remains open.

This practice of using various texts as extra-liturgical material for motets as Mass, particularly the accompaniment of the Elevation and Communion by motets with generally appropriate texts, is confirmed by the table of contents of the Modenese composer Gemignano Capilupi's *Motectorum sex et octo vocibus* of 1603:

Table III.

Title	Occasion
Vidi speciosam	BVM at any time
Egredimini	BVM at any time
Iste est panis	Eucharist, Corpus Christi
Dominator Domine	In time of prayer
Ecce agnus	Passiontide
Lauda Jerusalem Dominum	BVM
Omnis terra adoret te	Elevation
Ego sum panis	Eucharist
Suscipe me Domine	At any time
Confitemini Domino	At any time
Domini est terra	At any time
Afferte Domino	Sacrament
Laetentur caeli	Nativity
Surrexit Christus	Easter

Table III. (*cont.*)

Title	*Occasion*
Salve radix	BVM
Cantate Domino	At any time
O Domine libera	For the dead
Omnes servi	St. Sebastian
In hac sacra	Corpus Christi
Adoramus te Christe	Elevation
Pange lingua	Processions
Triumphalis	St. Laurence
O beatum pontificem	S. Gemignano [patron of Modena Cathedral]
Congratulamini	BVM

The list also supports the contention that texts were used rather loosely: Mass Propers like *Laetentur caeli*, the Offertory for Christmas Day, are suitable as general motet material, and single psalm verses such as *Domini est terra* and *Confitemini Domino* may be used throughout the year. Nor does Capilupi simply specify feasts; for two of the texts he indicates a position in the Mass – the Elevation. The text *Adoramus te Christe* can be identified as a responsory for Good Friday, but apparently it was widely sung as an Elevation motet. Another composer, Andrea Bianchi, designated both this text and *O sacrum convivium* for the Elevation in his Masses and motets of 1611.

The psalm and Magnificat antiphons at Vespers provided many texts for composers all over northern Italy. In its plainsong form, such an antiphon was sung both before and after its psalm or Magnificat, according to the rubrics (it also set the mode for it). Where the antiphon text was set to measured music, however, it was probably sung in this form at the end only, especially if the plainsong setting had been sung before, as mentioned above (page 158, note 22). Magnificat antiphons in particular were set frequently, for since the Magnificat assumes greater solemnity than the psalms sung earlier in the Office, composers tended to accord its antiphon the dignity of a musical setting more often than those of psalms. Even so, the feasts from whose texts Grandi, Viadana, and others chose form a random selection from the liturgical calendar; not on every Sunday or feastday could a church-goer expect to hear a specially composed antiphon at Vespers. The incidence of antiphon settings was certainly less haphazard than that of Mass Propers, however, and the former seem much more likely to have been intended for their correct liturgical place, even if – as we have seen – substitution was practised as an alternative. In any case, Vespers was often carried out with greater solemnity than Mass, to judge from the comparative profusion of elaborate, sometimes massively scored settings of large portions of the Vespers liturgy.

A surprising statistic revealed in Table I, but one by no means untypical of a wider sample of composers, is the high proportion of texts belonging to the responsories of Matins. There is no indication that this Office was generally performed chorally in the early seventeenth century except at Christmas and in Holy Week, so why the popularity of responsory texts? The reason must be that composers, anxious to enlarge their quarry of suitable textual material for any given feast or day, felt able to extend their choice to the many texts in their liturgical books appertaining to Offices other than those normally sung chorally. Such texts would have been quite appropriate for either antiphon substitute or extra-liturgical motet material at Mass or Vespers. For example, the text *Quem vidistis pastores*, set by several composers, is a responsory at Matins on Christmas Day: what better motet text for general use on the great feast, with its reference to the biblical narrative?[30]

Table IV shows the list of feasts and Sundays whose liturgical texts Grandi selected for motets:

Table IV. *Feasts providing texts for Grandi's motets*
(one setting except where indicated in parentheses)

Proper of the Time	St. John the Baptist (24 June)
First Sunday of Advent	Assumption (15 Aug.) (6)
First Monday of Advent	Nativity of BVM (8 Sep.)
Nativity (3)	St. Michael (29 Sep.)
Circumcision	St. Jerome (30 Sep.)
Fourth Sunday after Epiphany	St. Ursula (21 Oct.)
Ash Wednesday	All Saints (1 Nov.) (2)
Holy Week	St. Caecilia (22 Nov.) (2)
Fifth Sunday after Easter	
Sunday after Ascension	*Common of the Saints*
Pentecost (5)	Apostles
Saturday after Pentecost	Martyrs (3)
Trinity	Confessor Bishops
Corpus Christi (4)	Virgins (2)
Proper of the Saints	Dedication of a church
St. Silvester (31 Dec.)	Of the BVM
St. Anthony (17 Jan.)	For the propagation of the faith (3)
St. Sebastian (20 Jan.)	For peace
Annunciation (25 Mar.) (4)	For the sick
Finding of the Cross (3 May) (3)	For the Trinity

As we have seen, there is no particular emphasis on one type of feast, and the selection covers many occasions in the Church year. Since Grandi's choice is quite typical of the period, the table gives a fairly representative picture. Even in big cities like Venice, there seems to have been little differentiation between small and large feasts in respect of motet texts; on grand occasions, the additional dignity and ceremony would have been provided musically by large-scale psalm and Magnificat settings. Of course, St. Mark's had a tradition of daily music, so that motets for lesser feasts on weekdays had a chance of performance in the correct liturgical position. Grandi's four books of motets published in the 1620s (omitted in the preparation of Table IV as well as Table I earlier) introduce motets for two such feasts, St. Lucy and S. Rocco. Earlier, in the days of the Gabrielis, however, splendour had taken the form of polychoral motets usually set to texts appropriate only to great feasts.[31] Texts from the liturgy of Corpus Christi seem to have been popular with composers – Grandi wrote a number of motets upon them – and it is quite likely that these were also intended for general use in honour of the Eucharist or at the Elevation, as has been mentioned. Texts like O *salutaris hostia* and O *sacrum convivium* stand on the borderline between liturgical usage and 'spiritual recreation', the idea developed by the Jesuits during the Counter-Reformation era.

'Spiritual recreation' in its broad sense may well have been the function composers envisaged for their settings of non-liturgical texts. As we have already seen, this concept was first introduced in the 1560s by the Oratorians under St. Philip Neri at Rome; their music was set to sacred vernacular texts. Its devotional spirit was entirely consistent with the ideals of the Council of Trent, which ended in 1563. Even secular tunes had their words subtly altered for sacred use.[32] Collections such as the Florentine Serafino Razzi's first book of *Laude spirituali* (1563) were sung not only in monasteries and convents but also at social gatherings and in private homes.[33] This last use was also envisaged by composers in the seventeenth century, especially in cities with a flourishing court and social life: title-pages proclaimed the suitability of their more intimate concertato music for performance in 'princely apartments' as well as in church.[34] The borderline between Latin and vernacular devotional texts was often difficult to define, and collections sometimes contained music set to both languages. Patta's *Motetti et madrigali* (1614) consists of Latin motets interspersed with spiritual madrigals marked *pietosi affetti* to Italian texts by the dedicatee, Abbot Angelo Grillo, while Pietro Pace's 1619 motets have vernacular arias for solo voice and continuo corresponding to the words of each Latin motet. These arias appear only in the continuo part, suggesting secular performance by a singer looking over the continuo, or accompanying himself on lute or spinet. One of the Latin texts, *Quid prodest stulto* ('What does it profit a man to be rich?') is typical of the moral tone of some spiritual madrigals.

Whereas Viadana viewed the solo motet from a purely 'practical' angle, that is, as a medium of the utmost simplicity for use where choristers were in short supply, Monteverdi and others (especially in a city like Mantua) saw it as a medium conducive to the singer's own spiritual enjoyment and benefit. Even so, the distinction between the style of vernacular spiritual and Latin non-liturgical pieces was small. Jacopo Peri's little aria *I miei giorni fugaci* (text by Rinuccini) has a melodic line as uncomplicated as that of the simplest Viadana motet.[35] That much Latin music for one or few voices could be sung in secular surroundings is demonstrated by the plethora of title-pages indicating the harpsichord, lute and *chitarrone* as alternative continuo instruments.[36] This would happen in some cities more than others, and it is clear that solo motets were widely sung in church, following Viadana's lead. In a large centre like Venice, domestic performance would have been more frequent; Grandi's three volumes of solo and duet motets with violins, the majority of whose texts were non-liturgical, were published after he had moved there. The inclusion of several spiritual madrigals at the beginning of Monteverdi's *Selva morale* testifies to the continuing popularity of spiritual recreation in the Venice of the 1640s, and indeed the very title of the collection suggests that it contains music for personal devotion as well as for liturgical use.

Settings of parts of the Song of Songs were a prominent feature among the extra-liturgical motets. The Song of Songs was a well-explored quarry for composers of the more sensuous type of motet, for it was the nearest biblical text to the love-poetry of the period; this affinity seems to have attracted composers, particularly those experienced in the secular field. Nevertheless, these texts are not as liturgically unsuitable as we might imagine; brief extracts from the Song of Songs occur in the Office as antiphons on many Marian feasts, and any settings from this source could have been considered suitable for such feasts, even if they did not correspond exactly to the texts prescribed. They could have been used, too, on feasts of female saints, especially virgins.[37] The amorous undertones of these texts brought forth some of the composers' best music. In contrast to secular settings, passion was subdued in this music; it was sublimated and transfigured in the cause of a religious fervour that was redolent of the Jesuits, and more inflamed than the simple devotion of the Oratorians. As for other non-liturgical texts, most consist of devotions – sometimes non-biblical and with poetic interpolations – to Our Lord, to the Virgin, or to a particular saint, and would have been suitable for singing as motets at Mass if performed in church. One could include under this heading the settings of isolated psalm verses which reflect a mood and could have been sung at an appropriate liturgical season – e.g. melancholy psalm verses in Lent, joyous ones at Eastertide.

Although composers in northern Italy as a whole did not set to music a very large proportion of strictly liturgical texts in their motets, it could in no way be said that they had lost any awareness of liturgical propriety. The advent of the *stile moderno*, with its greater emphasis on the expression of the words and the mood of the text, enhanced rather than detracted from the truly liturgical nature of church music. The grief of the Good Friday liturgy is perhaps nowhere more movingly expressed than in Grandi's motet *O vos omnes* (see Ex. 19, pp. 83–4) for solo soprano, three viols, and continuo: a scoring that defies the conventional ban on instruments during Lent, and might have courted disapproval from those later purists who frowned on any solo singing in a liturgical context. In the sense that it conveys and expresses the words beautifully and simply, this is real 'liturgical' music, and it is one among many examples. Within the fairly loose framework of current liturgical practice, we can see how, in general terms, early seventeenth-century composers attempted to provide a variety of church music throughout the Church year.

∙❧❧❧∙

The Musical Transition around 1600

THE last decades of the sixteenth century witnessed a decline of the strict polyphonic style in Italian sacred music, and the rise of several technical procedures that became standard in the baroque era. Though polyphony had, it is true, survived the strictures of the Council of Trent, the reforming spirit that flowed from the Council had the effect, albeit indirect, of undermining the purity of its style and of hastening its ultimate decline. The musical aim that words should be intelligible tied in, of course, with generally-held humanist views; the changes necessitated by this, though almost as far-reaching as Cranmer's one-note-to-a-syllable dictum of the Anglican Reformation, were much more slow-moving.

A particular candidate for stylistic simplification was the most liturgically important form of polyphonic art, the Mass. Not only had the words to be made comprehensible, but settings of the longer sections, Gloria and Credo, must be shortened; hence the concept of the *Missa brevis*. Chordal writing, by obviating the imitative process, quickly disposed of long stretches of text and made the words intelligible at the same time. Block chords could even occur at the opening of a movement, as in the Gloria of Palestrina's *Missa brevis*. Emphasis on the words at the expense of polyphonic elaboration caused composers to write syllabically and to exploit ideas that were rhythmic rather than melodic, even when not treated in chordal fashion. Chordal writing led to the use of contrasted sonorities, especially in works for five or more voices, and to the lively cross-accents often found in triple-time passages. All these non-polyphonic elements are present in Palestrina's later Masses, which are more clearly forward-looking in style than many have previously supposed.[1] There is an affinity between them and contemporary Venetian music; Andrea Gabrieli's *Missa brevis* (c. 1580), for example, has much chordal writing resulting in harmonic bass lines.[2] Even in Victoria's Masses, where the polyphony usually remains more pure, a tendency towards homophony is evident in more richly-scored works – the *Missa Vidi speciosam* for example.

Another factor in the decline of polyphony in the late sixteenth century which is all too easily overlooked is the widespread practice of ornamenting church music in performance. Modern 'straight' performances of Palestrina Masses may well fail to recreate the authentic sound of this music as heard in the Italy of the 1580s. It did not need the birth of opera to call forth vocal virtuosity; this was already a speciality of Italian singers, in churches as much as at courts. The practice of ornamentation was codified in the writings of men like the Venetians Giovanni Bassano and Girolamo Dalla Casa and the Milanese Giovanni Battista Bovicelli in the last decades of the century. Within the framework of certain conventions, singers were given free rein to improvise elaborate vocal patterns from simple polyphonic ideas.[3] Lavish ornament sung by one soloist only could be abused; the more moderate procedure was for various individual singers from each section of the choir to take turns in ornamenting their own parts, as in Bassano's example of a madrigal in which the soprano and bass alternately add elaboration to their lines.[4] A study of the ornaments he suggests shows that when these were tastefully applied the music need not suffer drastic change. By contrast, Bovicelli's suggestions for really complex, almost non-rhythmic ornament were extreme, and cannot have been the norm in church music, for few choirs would have had the soloists to do them justice; in any case, by ignoring the total texture, they destroyed the original music. Nevertheless, the very concept of singling out one part of the texture to be sung by a soloist was anti-polyphonic, and led naturally to the infiltration of the 'melody and bass' idea of the Baroque into choral music. It was all part of a process whereby the vertical elements of music, rhythm and harmony, slowly undermined the horizontal, melody and counterpoint. For when the music was in general vertically conceived, as for instance in the Gloria of Palestrina's *Missa Assumpta est Maria*, an ornamented part would not destroy but rather tend to enrich the musical sense.

The growth of homophonic writing and the exploitation of sonority together led to a new interest in harmonic colour and modulation on the part of a number of north Italian church composers before 1600. Harmonically conceived music, whether for few voices or for double-choir scorings, encouraged the decay of the modal system and an awareness of the possibilities of key contrasts, even though the establishment of a fully worked-out tonal system was still a long way off. In Ruffo's *Adoramus te*, a short chordal motet, frequent chords of G minor lend the basic A minor tonality a 'dark', Phrygian colour, and their distance from the dominant harmonies of E major creates fascinating tensions. There was nothing new about Phrygian progressions and cadences, of course, but here Ruffo seems to be exploring their harmonic asperities in a novel way, especially in the final chord sequence, G minor – A major – E major. Even composers whose polyphonic writing was more conservative could show an interest in harmonic colour. Asola's *Missa pro defunctis* for ATTB contains a mixture of imitative and chordal styles but, in the *Dies irae* especially, resorts to austere harmonies which suggest the mood of the words in a most madrigalian manner; the close scoring produces a rich sonority.[5] In Ingegneri's motet *O Domine Jesu* there are chord juxtapositions such as C/E flat and C minor/A minor, the first of which at least is not caused by contrapuntal interplay. In

Orazio Vecchi's eight-part *Missa pro defunctis*, the *Dies irae* has alternate
verses sung by each of the two choirs and, though not lacking imitation,
relies on an austere harmonic idiom, as in Asola's Requiem; false relations,
unusual modulations, and complex harmonies caused by passing notes all
play their part.[6] Chordal verses are punctuated by general pauses, for
dramatic effect, while the low tessitura of the second choir adds sombre
colour.

   A kind of polyphony quite different from Palestrina's is exemplified by
the Bolognese Ascanio Trombetti's motet *Paratum cor meum* (1589).[7] Here
the emphasis is on the distinctive character of the musical ideas clothing the
successive sections of text: 'cantabo' is conveyed by a melisma with hints of
sequence, 'et psalmum dicam' by a bustling figure in close imitation, and
'exsurge' by ponderous minims treated antiphonally between pairs of
voices. This sort of contrast was to become an important feature of the
concertato motet of the early seventeenth century, in which continuity of
texture gave place to a greater feeling of sectionalization. It led naturally to
the appearance of another new technical device in the last years of the
sixteenth century; the introduction of repeated material and refrain schemes
for the sake of coherent musical structure. We can observe this practice in a
six-part motet by Giovanni Bassano, *Dic nobis Maria* (1598), where the
opening chordal passage occurs three times as a refrain, and the central
triple-time episode is repeated before the final Alleluia.[8] Such procedures
were on the whole less usual in smaller textures than in polychoral ones,
where they were employed in particular by Giovanni Gabrieli, as we shall
see later.

   The stylistic changes outlined so far are epitomized in the Masses and
motets of the Venetian Giovanni Croce. The former belong to the *Missa
brevis* type; in the first *Missa sexti toni*, chordal writing dispatches long
stretches of text in economical fashion, with voices entering at close
intervals if not in pairs. From the homophonic opening of the two-part
verset 'Et iterum' in the Credo it is but a short step to the two-part motets of
Viadana with their *basso continuo*. Croce's use of strongly accented triple
time anticipates the concertato idiom, as in *Beati eritis*, where one such
passage consists rhythmically of a free succession of 3/4, 3/2 and 6/4 bars (in
reduced values), according to the accentuation of the text.[9] Canonic entry at
short distances, another device beloved of the early concertato composers,
occurs in *Ego sum pauper,* while in *Cantate Domino* Croce exploits
key-relationships, repeatedly affirming G minor at cadences only to end the
motet with a striking, and contradictory, close in C major.

   The increasing interest in the vertical aspects of music had worked against
the polyphonic style, and encouraged composers to develop a sense of
modulation, clear verbal declamation, and mood painting; ornamentation
had militated against counterpoint. Though all these tendencies pointed
towards a new style, they did not in themselves add up to one. In

non-polychoral music, composers had yet to achieve contrasts of texture and colour; apart from brief interludes, most church music just before 1600 remained in four or more parts. In this context, Antonio Mortaro's three-part *Sacrae cantiones* of 1598 are unusually prophetic, for almost all the pieces are trios for two upper voices and bass in a style that bridges the gap between the light, often three-part, *madrigaletto* of the 1580s and the true concertato duet. The existence of a score, headed *partitione*, indicates that such music was accompanied by the organ. Here was the sort of music in which the practice of ornamentation need not lead to a cul-de-sac, for it would no longer be a show of virtuosity based on ideas originally conceived for a different purpose. Only a new texture would encourage a melodic style of vocal writing conceived in terms of ornament, which had been inhibited by the preoccupation with harmony and the continuous use of four or more voices: Mortaro led the way, but the principal figure to break new ground in tackling the problem was Viadana.

Viadana's Cento concerti ecclesiastici

The first volume of Viadana's *Cento concerti* appeared in the same year, 1602, as that most important document of Florentine monody, Caccini's *Le nuove musiche*, and in its own field its appearance was just as significant. But though the fundamental inspiration of the stylistic changes of which it was the natural outcome might have been a generally humanist spirit, the changes themselves had much less to do with the Florentine *Camerata* than historians used to assume. In the small cities of northern Italy, new ideas arose out of practical exigencies rather than high-flown theorizing like that of the Florentines. It was to the problems of singing in small provincial cathedrals or collegiate churches with limited resources that Viadana addressed himself in publishing the *Cento concerti*. Rather than give an inadequate performance of conventional polyphony in four or more parts, which required a fairly large choir probably with instrumental support, he preferred to devise a kind of church music using a few solo voices and giving the organ a specific accompanying role enshrined in the ostensibly new concept of the *basso continuo*. Though ostensibly new, it actually arose out of the *basso seguente* practice already well established, and entirely appropriate to the vertical orientation of so much late sixteenth-century church music. The concept of *basso continuo* was an extension of this earlier practice, for the organist now became leader of the ensemble, providing a full harmony and ← contributing to the musical argument where the voices had rests. It made possible the development of the small-scale concertato style of the early seventeenth century.

Having said that, it may be as well to examine first the four-part motets of the *Cento concerti*, which have the most conventional scoring – though they offer, given the independent continuo, the greatest possibility of textural variety. Throughout the survey,[10] we shall be looking for evidence of concern for musical structure in the wake of the abandonment of conventional polyphony, but while we may expect to come across experiments with refrain forms, especially in the four-part motets, we shall find that by no means all of them have any balanced design at all. *O sacrum convivium* is one such motet; the triple-time section does not act as a refrain but is an isolated passage, as in many sixteenth-century motets, and the continuo is merely a *basso seguente*.[11] This setting belongs to a number of pieces for low voices whose texture, though generally old-fashioned and lacking in contrast, offers possibilities of rich harmonic sonority. These Viadana grasps in another similar motet, *Quis dabit capiti meo*, which has several telling chromatic progressions and unexpected chords.[12] In another motet lacking an overall design, *Jam de somno*, the interest is provided by the fashionable device of echo, a characteristic of some early baroque motets; the echoes, at the ends of phrases in all four voices, are shown by capital letters in the underlay, and the effect of half-words (*implora/plora*, *clama/ama* etc.) is fully exploited.

Of the four-part motets with some formal scheme, a number have the basic ternary shape *ABA*, but it is the extended rondo forms that show the greatest variety of texture. *Dic Maria*, for instance, has a triple-time tutti alternating with solo sections for each of the four voices in turn – one of the earliest appearances in church music of a refrain form that was to be popular among composers using forces both large and small, for sharing out the solo work not only achieved variety but was fairer to the singers. In the strophic hymn *Sanctorum meritis*, Viadana lays the music out in the form *ABACA*, each section covering one verse. The refrain is in triple time but reverses the conventional rhythm of (in modern values) 3/4 bars with a hemiola at the cadence, by having a basic hemiola rhythm (♩ ♩ ♩ | ♫♩ 𝄾) with a 6/4 bar (𝅗𝅥 ♩ ♩ ♩) at each cadence. This is not the only time Viadana departs from convention in his triple rhythms, for in the refrain of *Cantabant Sancti* he has sturdy dotted patterns, which imply a dignified tempo prophetic of the mid-baroque aria. Strophic hymn texts may, of course, invite a strophic setting, as in *Diei solennia*. A rondo form with interludes, as in *Dic Maria*, unifies *Congregati sunt inimici nostri*, whose refrain is distinguished not by triple metre but by a crisp chordal style, and whose interludes contrast pairs of voices. *Gaude Virgo* marks a tentative approach towards variation form, an important new step. Its bass is given four statements (varied slightly on the second appearance), above each of which two SB groups alternately sing a duet, leading to a tutti which stays the same throughout. A more typical formal device is the Alleluia refrain, as in *Repleatur*, scored not for four voices but for AT and two trombones – an early instance of the composer specifying instruments, even if the parts are still vocal in style. An altogether more novel texture, unique among Viadana's four-part motets, is found in

Filiae Jerusalem, a trio for three equal sopranos and bass doubled by continuo, parallel in layout to Luzzaschi's madrigals of 1601 or Giovanni Gabrieli's *Sonata a tre violini*. Its Alleluia is not a refrain but a repeated section (making the form of the motet *ABCC*) and consists of falling root-position harmonies over a remarkable sweeping bass line [Ex. 1]. Here the feverish bustle of the imitative upper voices is suggestive of instrumental writing and anticipates the violin figurations of the sonatas and motet *sinfonie* of several decades later: Viadana excels in this motet, whose character is firmly seventeenth-century.

Ex. 1. Viadana, *Filiae Jerusalem*

Viadana's aim in the four-part motets of the *Cento concerti* was to simplify style further than his immediate predecessors such as Orazio Vecchi and Asola had done, and to eliminate complexity from church music. In the two- and three-part motets he broke, once and for all, the stranglehold of the four-part texture by reducing the number of voices and increasing the importance of the organ continuo. Nevertheless, the two-part pieces at least remained anachronistic in style, for in most of them the lower part was doubled by the organ; omit the organ, and they turn out to be little different from the two-part versets of, say, Lassus or even Josquin, being largely imitative or canonic. They are like Viadana's single-voice motets with the bass line vocalized. An example is *Sub tuum praesidium* for soprano and alto, in which the continuo, far from supporting a duet of high voices, actually doubles the alto part and is written in the alto clef; the only concessions to modernity are the flowing movement of the triple-time passage and an elaborately ornamented cadence in the upper part.[13] Among these old-fashioned settings, there are one or two true duets, such as *Laetare Jerusalem* for two sopranos, which opens like a *bicinium*, with a *basso seguente* following the lowest sounding part, but soon becomes a three-part texture.[14] Signs of a new treatment of the medium here include repeated rhythms, and falling 6/3 chords at 'tristitia', an apt piece of word painting; it is noticeable that the bass line, freed from doubling voices, moves more quickly and functions more harmonically. Another true duet, *Misericordias Domini*, has a rounded ternary form with the outer passages in triple time; the inner section contains an example of repeated tonic-dominant harmony, with the two voices interweaving, that became common in certain baroque music of a triumphal type, and which was a symptom of the growing awareness of tonal feeling at this stage. Viadana also set the ubiquitous text *Duo seraphim* in the usual dialogue fashion and, in order to satisfy conventional musical symbolism, required the organist to sing a third part at the words 'tres sunt qui testimonium dant'.

It is in the three-part motets that Viadana achieves a more consistently modern style. As before, the lowest voice doubles the continuo, which leaves the two upper voices free to interweave a characteristically baroque duet texture. The low voice is not always a bass: in *Jubilate Deo* the scoring is SSA. Marks of a conventional style – trumpet motives for the words 'in sono tubae' and melismatic cadence passages – can be found here and there, but many newer ideas appear; affective chromaticism redolent of the monodists in *O Jesu mi dulcissime* [Ex. 2], double echoes in *Ingredere* (here

Ex.2. Viadana, *O Jesu mi dulcissime*

cadences are repeated *piano* by a distant voice and *pianissimo* by an even more distant one), and instrumental scoring in *O bone Jesu* (written for tenor and two trombones, doubtless a most appropriate combination in churches that had instrumentalists on their payrolls). Perhaps the most interesting single piece is *Fili, quid fecisti*, which belongs to the genre of the Latin dramatic dialogue, a forerunner of oratorio.[15] The text narrates the biblical story of the Finding in the Temple, with the three voices representing respectively Jesus, Mary, and Joseph; after the section in dialogue, Viadana recapitulates the entire text in a setting for the three voices together, as if he were unsure that the realistic dramatic part of the motet could stand on its own. The style of the music is conventional compared to later Latin dialogues; it is the idea of representing characters by solo voices that is new in the sacred repertory.

In these three-part motets, refrain and rondo forms are, once again, of particular interest. The simplest method of giving musical coherence to pieces that no longer relied upon polyphonic imitation was to have an Alleluia refrain where the text suggested it, in a style contrasted with that of the rest of the piece – as in *Non turbetur*, where the Alleluia is based on descending sequence patterns like those in some of Monteverdi's madrigals (Viadana worked at Mantua while Monteverdi was there).[16] The motet *Fili mi Absalom*, for SST, is one of the few in regular rondo form. The opening material is in triple time, and is slightly varied on its second appearance.[17] The scheme that Viadana seems to prefer, however, is one that involves repetition not of the opening music but of later sections – *ABB* or *ABCBC*. Again, the sections may be distinguished by time signature; or they may be signalled by the recurrence of a motto theme, as in *Venite et videte*, cast in the *ABB* mould with the opening three words carrying the repeated idea.[18] The motet *O quam pulchra es* [Ex. 3a & b] illustrates the *ABCBC* scheme, and possesses a number of modern features – many ascending and descending sequences in the manner of Monteverdi, contrast between long and short note-values, and a charming conflict of rhythm and harmony at the Alleluia. The manipulation of note-lengths is especially striking at the opening, where regularity of metre is in doubt till the orthodox cadence at the fifth bar. The generally madrigalian feeling of this music is no

Ex.3(a & b). Viadana, *O quam pulchra es*

surprise, for the text comes from the Song of Songs. It is in a motet like this that Viadana achieves a progressive duet style; the bass is admittedly vocalized by the lowest voice, but it could be omitted without great injustice being done to the musical content. This is precisely what Viadana's followers did, for the true concertato duet, with equal voices interweaving or singing in thirds, tended to assume an independent, slow-moving bass line from which contrapuntal interest had been all but banished. In trio motets with a bass voice, they would give the bass a solo section, or at least some measure of independence to avoid its being completely subservient to the continuo.

Ex. 3(b)

The solo motets of the *Cento concerti* are the ones that break the newest ground historically, for they are the first published liturgical music for forces that had been pared down to the bare minimum – one voice and organ. Viadana devised this medium not out of any revolutionary intent, but (so he claimed) as the ultimate solution to the problems of small choirs with a handful of singers incapable of doing justice to conventional polyphony. Although it is true that such music could be transformed by the addition of ornamentations by a more experienced singer, Viadana himself hardly made any stylistic advance in the solo motets. Their vocal line seems little more than the upper part of a four-part texture, of which the remainder is supplied by organ rather than voices. From this point of view they resemble the English lute air, which could be sung either in four parts or as a solo with lute accompaniment; the lute writing changed only slowly from being a kind of transcription of three voice parts to having its own idiomatic style. Replace Viadana's organ part with voices, and the music would sound little different from a genuine four-part motet like *O sacrum convivium*. This impression is strengthened by the regularity with which voice and bass move together. Viadana's word painting is often conventional – for instance, the falling octave in both parts to paint the word 'grief' in *Versa est in luctum*. There are, however, occasional hints of influence from the new monodic style, as at the beginning and end of *Super flumina*, where a sluggish bass line and characteristic *trillo* ornaments are used [Ex. 4]. Several pieces have some kind of formal scheme – an Alleluia refrain or some other

Ex. 4. Viadana, *Super flumina*

repeated triple-time passage, or an *ABCBC* layout, as in the last-mentioned motet. Sometimes Viadana varies the pace of the music to match the mood of the text. A good example of the unadventurous quality of the solo motets as a whole is *Exaudi me Domine*, with its very active, purely harmonic bass line, often moving with the voice, but from time to time leading an imitation.[19] The only musical development consists of repeating certain vocal phrases with perhaps a varied bass or a longer cadence – variations on the very simplest level.

The bass solo motets stand apart from the rest, and are musically undistinguished in every way. For the most part the voice doubles the continuo, pausing only to take breath while the latter introduces a new idea.[20] In bringing the voice in a fourth or fifth higher than the organ entry, Viadana attempts to preserve some vestige of the old imitative technique as a bare minimum of musical interest. Without an organist capable of extemporizing keyboard figurations or some kind of contrapuntal texture, such interest must have of necessity been at a premium, and it is perhaps odd that in motets which have abandoned all sense of organized contrapuntal elaboration, there are no compensating attempts at rounded musical structures. That Viadana could occasionally burst free from this constricted style is evident from the remarkable two-octave run that concludes *Misereor super turbam*; scalic runs are a common form of ornament in bass motets. The only bass motet with a voice part independent of the continuo is *O Jesu dulcis*, but here the voice is marked *baritonus*.

Although historically important, the solo motets are the least musically promising of Viadana's *Cento concerti*. The solo motet was soon to become established in northern Italy, but Viadana failed to realize its formal or stylistic potential, for he conceived it as the result of a ruthless paring down of part-music. He achieved far more significant changes of style in some of his three- and four-part motets, by experimenting with various kinds of balanced musical form, and by bringing a fresh approach to matters of scoring and rhythm to bear upon a simple, practically-conceived music. The solo motets were novel in scoring but not in style, partly because Viadana was writing for comparatively inexperienced singers who could not have executed the more elaborate ornaments of Caccini and his followers, and partly because the solo part lacks sufficient melodic distinction. Few of the two-part pieces anticipate the modern duet style which, as composers soon realized, did not require a vocalized bass line; as has been shown, this style had to be sought among Viadana's three-part works. His bass-voice parts are more continuously wedded to the continuo line than was later to be the case. Viewed as a whole, their fast-moving bass lines (this is a remarkably consistent feature) and lack of declamatory writing give the *Cento concerti* a somewhat restless style. Nevertheless, despite all their conservative elements, they undoubtedly mark an important stage in the evolution of the few-voiced concertato motet. They provide a complete change from, almost a corrective to, massive multi-choral church music, and in this sense they redress the musical balance around 1600. By fusing selected features in this music with the declamatory and melodic writing of the monodists, we have the makings of much of the small-scale Italian church music for several decades to come.

The sixteenth-century cori spezzati *style*

The complexities of large-scale church music in the early Baroque can be traced back to one simple device: the use of *cori spezzati*, separated choirs. In works in six or fewer parts, clarity of texture was possible without the division of the choir; contrast between groupings of voices was certainly exploited, but it was necessarily informal and constantly changing (as, for example in five-part pieces where contrasted three-part groupings were possible only if one part belonged to both). In works for eight voices, the choir was formally divided into two balanced SATB units (at first) and the age-old antiphonal style held sway, by which the composer played off one choir against the other, reserving the use of the full eight-part tutti for climaxes by way of contrast. This technique enshrines two levels of contrast fundamental to the large-scale church music of the early Baroque: first, contrast between one choir and another, between distinct groups; second, contrast between individual groups and the tutti. If the word 'voice' is substituted for 'group', these are of course exactly the same levels of contrast that characterize the few-voiced concertato – a substitution which succinctly demonstrates the difference of approach in large-scale music. Because in *cori spezzati* writing the more intimate contrapuntal argument of few-voiced music is replaced by the emphasis on groups, there is a prevalence of block harmony in it; sonority is more important than counterpoint.

Since too much attention has been paid to the contrapuntal aspects of sixteenth-century church music – especially when studying it as a compositional discipline – the historical importance of *cori spezzati* used perhaps to be underestimated. Moreover, it was a more widespread practice geographically than was often assumed; though more predominant and in the end, more fully developed in Venice than anywhere else, it was by no means an exclusively Venetian phenomenon. The works of Palestrina, Victoria, and Lassus provide many examples; and, owing to Germany's comparative closeness to Venice and to Lassus's position at the Munich court, the practice was popular with German composers such as Jacob Handl and Hassler.[21] By the turn of the century, huge anthologies of Italian double-choir motets were appearing in both Catholic and Protestant parts of Germany.

Let us examine some features of Palestrina's and Victoria's *cori spezzati* works. The openings may often be indistinguishable from those of a normal four-part motet with their imitative entries for one choir, though this exposition may be repeated by the second choir, introducing the spatial element into the music. Phrases become progressively shorter until a fairly swift alternation of the choirs is reached. The bass line is harmonic in function, while other voices have smoother contours; in the tutti, polyphony may become complex in the inner parts. Triple-time sections appear frequently, having simple rhythms and strong accents, and with the choirs overlapping closely. In his eight-part music, Lassus preferred brilliant polyphonic interweaving of parts to simple chordal writing, and tended to ignore the variety of phrase-lengths and the contrasts of colour that can be observed in the works of Venetian and Roman composers.

It was in the area around Venice rather than in the city itself that the first school of composers of *cori spezzati* music had sprung up in the early years of the sixteenth century.[22] Their works were additionally interesting for being precocious examples of the complete psalm setting, which Willaert at St. Mark's continued to develop in his psalms for separated choirs, though his manner was more severe and controlled, avoiding the frequent alternations between the choirs and the brilliant dialogue of the early composers.[23] His practice, codified by the theorist Zarlino, of making each choir harmonically complete, so that a listener nearer one choir than the other should still hear a satisfactory chord, was a good principle, though one which Lassus, in his quest for brilliance of sonority, did not appreciate. At St. Mark's, Andrea Gabrieli continued to expand the possibilities of the polychoral style, enlarging the musical forces to three choirs and writing for groups of varying tessitura. In his twelve-part Magnificat the first choir consists of SSAA, the second of SATB, and the third of ATTB; the total pitch range is well over three octaves.[24] The work is made up of phrases of varied length passed in overlapping entries from choir to choir, the whole ensemble combining from time to time in a sonorous tutti. Unlike the Roman brand of double-choir writing, polyphony is limited here to a few inner passing notes; simple chordal textures, whose musical interest is purely harmonic, suffice for the most part. The Kyrie, with sections in five, eight, and twelve parts respectively, has passages written in a similar way.[25]

Of the forward-looking elements of the *cori spezzati* style, the most important was the essential idea of contrasts between groups and tutti. The predominance of block chordal writing, which characterizes this style even more than the few-voiced idiom, encouraged composers to be aware of the possibilities of harmony for its own sake – a sense of modulation and the dramatic juxtaposition of unrelated harmonies are but two elements arising from this transitional phase between the church modes and modern tonality.

Outside Venice, Adriano Banchieri's eight-part *Concerti ecclesiastici* of 1595 illustrate a forward-looking double-choir style of the 1590s. This is one of the earliest publications to have a separate organ part, containing the outer parts of Choir I as a clear indication of the harmony. A note to the organist indicates that 'the composer's intention is to have the music concerted for separate choirs'; this might mean that another similar organ part would need to be written out for the second choir, or that instrumental doubling might be used instead. Either way, it is likely that both choirs were accompanied, and indeed, that this had been the practice in northern Italy for many years. Such written-out organ parts merely consolidated an expedient habit that led naturally to the *basso continuo*.[26] The *concerti* themselves provide examples of repeated sections (the *ABB* scheme beloved of Viadana) and contrasts between smooth, mainly contrapuntal writing and vigorous homophony. Rhythmic interplay between blocks of voices is an important element in the style, and there are some typical pictorial devices at the words 'in voce tubae' in the Ascensiontide motet *Omnes gentes plaudite manibus* – rapidly overlapping triadic trumpet figures above a tonic pedal.[27] Such music as this is entirely characteristic of a vast corpus of functional motets printed in the last years of the sixteenth century.

How do Giovanni Gabrieli's earlier works contribute to this repertory? Many of the early *concerti* published in 1587 were generally polyphonic in concept, sonorously written in six or seven parts; but even here voices group themselves together into blocks to be played off against one another – the seeds of the concertato style. Other motets by Giovanni in this collection exploit the massive polychoral scorings developed by his uncle Andrea, often with two choirs of four, five, or six voices apiece. In this double-choir music, the basslines of each choir do not double each other at the unison or octave in tutti passages. There are two reasons for this: first, that Choir I was often of higher tessitura than Choir II, its lowest part being a tenor, and second, that simple harmonic antiphony was so much the rule that the tutti came to have a much more contrapuntal texture by way of contrast; the separation of choirs each with self-sufficient harmony was abandoned.

In the double-choir music of Gabrieli's *Sacrae symphoniae I* (1597), on the other hand, the basses of the two choirs cease to be independent contrapuntal lines; in the tuttis they now sing the same notes.[28] The mainly polyphonic approach is disappearing; fresh and lively syncopated rhythms are emphasized by the chordal scoring, and triple time, with its strong accents, appears in the context of an essentially harmonic texture, rather than contrasting with linear polyphony as in Palestrina and Victoria. It is often used in the joyous Alleluia refrains typical of Gabrieli's mature motets. On the matter of refrains, what of formal organization here? Just as with Viadana at the other end of the textural spectrum, the abandonment of polyphonic structures meant that new ways of unifying the music had to be found. Once again, the *ABB* scheme appears; the repetition of *B* usually has the choirs reversed. The refrain, often set to the word Alleluia, is a particularly characteristic unifying device, and sometimes Gabrieli may vary it by modulating (as in its third appearance in *Surrexit Pastor bonus*) or by changing its scoring (in *Plaudite* it is sung successively by Choir III, Choir I, Choirs I and II, and finally by all three).

Gabrieli's large-scale church music is the stylistic bridge from Renaissance to Baroque, resolving in masterly fashion the tensions between polychoral and polyphonic styles.[29] In the later works, there were to be important innovatory tendencies.

⊘⫝⫝⫝⊘

CHAPTER V

Small-scale Church Music (I)

VIADANA'S *Cento concerti* were less important for their intrinsic musical qualities than for the profound changes of style that they prompted, and from about 1605 onwards music for the same forces – from one to four voices with organ – began to pour from the Venetian publishing houses. The splendid and dignified aspects of the Counter-Reformation were set aside in the face of the need in many provincial churches for a small-scale, practical, and functional music, which urged scores of composers into print for the first time. Many of these new composers were at least as talented as Viadana; some were to win considerable popularity and even acclaim by the second decade of the century. In the main, they were exclusively church composers, whose music was at first influenced only marginally by opera. This possibility depended on which city they worked in; the strong presence of secular and operatic music in a city like Mantua would have helped to develop the necessary new approach to melody in church music which is just detectable in the most progressive of Viadana's *concerti*. Freshness of melody was now combined with polyphonic treatment, rhythmic interest, and mood expression, to produce the new manner of few-voiced concertato music, though sometimes the melodic aspect was unfortunately the poor relation. In order to survey the wealth of this music it is necessary to consider the introduction of obbligato instruments separately, and to subdivide the remaining body of one- to six-part works into two broad categories. The solo, duet and trio with continuo will be considered first, for they had the more novel texture and were of more far-reaching historical significance.

Works for one, two and three voices with continuo

Looking at the duets and trios of those who followed Viadana, we can see that some of them failed to realize the vocal possibilities of the new medium. Two collections to appear before 1610, Leone Leoni's *Sacri fiori* (1606) and Caterina Assandra's *Motetti* (1609), illustrate this. Assandra's only advance on Viadana in the SB duet *Jubilate Deo* is in the greater independence of the bass-voice part from the continuo; she also uses sequential harmonies already apparent in Viadana, and in Monteverdi's madrigals.[1] Formal plans like *A B B* appear in the Leoni duets, but the vocal writing is not particularly idiomatic; in the jaunty triple-time Alleluia of *Ego dormivi*, the two sopranos could each be the top voices of a four-part choir, and the result would be indistinguishable from Gabrieli.

The second decade of the century was dominated by the most sought-after composer of small motets, Grandi, whose first five volumes, published between 1610 and 1619, all ran into several editions. In 1610 he directed music at the *Accademia dello Spirito Santo* in Ferrara, a charitable confraternity of lay people who could afford to employ a small choir in their services, for which these works were conceived. In his duet and trio motets, Grandi often exploits polyphonic techniques rather than formal possibilities, favouring canon and imitation rather than attempting structural balance. But the polyphony has a certain freshness because it is made up of melodies that are good in themselves and able to stand alone. They do not require ornamentation – decorations are in any case usually written out. Polyphony is no longer the essence of the music as in Palestrina; it is a means of developing self-sufficient solo melodies. That Grandi was a competent and assured master of the small motet by the time his first book of motets appeared in 1610 can be seen from the Christmas duet, *Hodie nobis de caelo*. Here he introduces an easily recognizable Alleluia refrain in triple time after the manner of Giovanni Gabrieli, and a motto idea for the word 'hodie' to begin each of the three stanzas. By giving the first stanza to the first voice, the second to the second voice, and the third to both in imitative interplay, Grandi has come much further than Viadana towards realizing the inherent contrasts that are possible even with just two equal voices.[2] The solo sections of this motet show the beginnings of a melodic style that was to lift Grandi's later works far above the level of many of his contemporaries.

By the time of Grandi's third book of motets (1614), polyphony was less important than formal design as a means of achieving musical variety. It tended to be abandoned completely in those occasional motets written for two or three bass voices, which sound rather like *cori spezzati* music reduced to its bare essentials – the harmony notes – with short phrases being passed between the voices. With the fourth book of motets (1616), Grandi realized the concept of extended melody without ornament over a varied bass line – plodding crotchets or long-held chords. Melodies are still announced by each voice in turn, but may be repeated in another key; they are developed by tonal manoeuvres and do not lose their force by repetition. The music, though tautly constructed, retains some of the spontaneity of recitative through its flexible rhythms and melodies. The duet *Surge propera* from this book illustrates the expressive vein in which Grandi responds to a characteristic Song of Songs text. Its SB scoring was second in popularity to the equal-voice duet; here we have come a long way from Viadana, however, for the bass voice is often independent of the continuo, and indeed the two voices sing in dialogue, as though between husband and wife – a conception strongly influenced by the secular and early operatic duet. Such personification was an exciting new possibility within the few-voiced medium. In *Surge propera*, the idea of human passion is expressed by a duet; the constant change of metre from a reflective 4/4 to an extrovert triple time is less an attempt at creating a strong formal structure than at delineating the ebb and flow of amorous feeling [Ex. 5]. The idiom of this motet points towards the thoroughly emotional, declamatory style more or less confined to secular music at that time (only Monteverdi, in the Vespers collection of 1610, had introduced it into church music with such abandon). Hitherto, the interest in imitative techniques had militated against excessive emotion or extended melody.

Ex. 5. Grandi, *Surge propera*

Grandi's mature duet style, and his achievements over the decade, are illustrated by *Anima Christi* for two tenors, from the fifth book of motets of 1619, entitled *Celesti fiori*. The text, a late medieval communion prayer, is very emotional and abounds in phrases of supplication. Once again, a very 'human' mode of expression reappears; the opening is a dialogue between the two voices, and much of the piece consists of finely controlled declamatory interplay. Grandi hardly touches the home key of G except at beginning and end; the shifting tonality conveys the waywardness of a soul without God. When only one of the voices is singing, Grandi adopts the chromatic alterations and written-out ornaments of the solo motet; on the other hand, the dissonant suspensions at 'let me not be separated from Thee' are among the most telling effects of the equal-voice duet.[3]

Countless other composers throughout the north Italian cities also adopted the 'small' concertato manner between 1610 and 1620. Giovanni Francesco Capello, one of the more important, included both dialogue[4] and echo duets in his *Sacrorum concentuum* of 1610; one of the duets (*Sancta et immaculata*) follows Viadana in that the second tenor often doubles the continuo, but its declamatory written-out *trillo* ornaments are quite up to date. Some composers gave the bass voice plenty of independence, and attempted some formal organization. Giovanni Battista Fergusio's *Motetti e dialoghi* (1612) are written in a competent florid manner with varied rhythms and harmonies, as at the bold opening of *Plorans et lacrimans* [Ex. 6]. But he has no real feel for melody; having evolved thematic ideas for short sections of text, he does nothing to develop them, and the ideas themselves are often too fragmentary to be capable of extension.

Ex.6. Fergusio, *Plorans et lacrimans*

A very good example of the comparatively rare scoring for a trio of sopranos is found in Ignazio Donati's *Non vos relinquam orphanos* (*Concerti ecclesiastici a2–5 voci*, 1618).[5] Donati was a much more capable melodist and could rival Grandi in his sure grasp of the style of the day. His trio is knit together by a delightfully varied Alleluia refrain over a downward-sweeping bass. The imitative passages punctuated by the refrain have exquisite part-writing, and a climax is reached after the sequential 'et gaudebit' stanza, built up by the rapid patterns of the bass line. *In te Domine speravi*, another motet from the same publication of 1618, whose text is the first three verses of Psalm 71, illustrates Donati's manner of duet writing – beautifully poised melodies announced and then treated in canon over a bass that is brisker than in Grandi [Ex. 7]. Donati achieves some measure of thematic coherence by extending or varying snatches of melody heard in the earlier part of the motet; one unobtrusive semiquaver figure is worked into an elaborate canonic cadenza at the close. Though Giovanni Paolo Caprioli lacks Donati's sustained melodic invention, the *Salve Regina* from his *Sacrae cantiones* (1618) is a fine example of the closely-knit yet freely declamatory duet, anticipating one of Monteverdi's treatments of the same text.

Ex.7. Donati, *In te Domine speravi*

Contrapuntal devices sustain the musical interest rather than melody itself, the bass line is varied in style, and some well-wrought triple counterpoint occurs at the chromatic 'gementes', where the 'in hac lacrimarum valle' phrase is freely inverted [Ex. 8].

Ex.8. Caprioli, *Salve Regina*

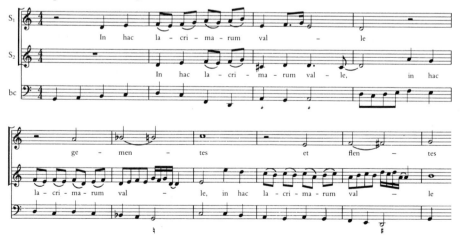

Let us now turn to the beginnings of the solo motet in the aftermath of Viadana's rather negative approach to the medium. His main contribution lay in proving its liturgical feasibility, and it was not long before the solo motet caught on with the more enterprising composers of the day. Although solo motets were at first far outnumbered by duets in published collections, and it was some time before composers' volumes and editors' anthologies of this particular kind of music began to appear (the first anthology was Leonardo Simonetti's *Ghirlanda sacra* of 1625), it is no longer possible to hold the view, expressed by Adrio, that the medium made an unusually late appearance in church music.[6] Of all the forms available to the composer of small-scale church music, ecclesiastical monody was the most appropriate to extra-liturgical use in secular surroundings. Thus, the publisher Vincenti listed several such collections under the heading of church music performable with stringed continuo instruments (harpsichord, *chitarrone, tiorba*) in his 1619 stock-catalogue. It is no surprise that many of their texts are from the Song of Songs (the one solo motet in Monteverdi's Vespers, *Nigra sum*, is an example). A large number of composers had acknowledged the rise of the new medium by including solo pieces in their collections of *concerti* during the ten years or so following Viadana's pioneering volume – for example Capello, Giovanni Paolo Cima, Antonio Burlini, Antonio Gualtieri, Ottavio Vernizzi, and Adriano Banchieri. The credit for the first publication solely of one-voice sacred pieces goes not to a northerner but to a Roman – Ottavio Durante (*Arie devote*, 1608); the first such northern publication was the first book of solo motets (1610) by Bartolomeo Barbarino, whose main reputation was as a writer of secular monodies. This was followed by the *Sacre laudi* of 1613 by Lodovico Bellanda, another practised monodist who followed fashion in suggesting the *chitarrone* as an alternative continuo instrument. His style in 4/4 is pleasant and recitative-like, with careful text declamation, occasional chromatic flats for expression, slow bass lines, and florid cadences; the short snatches of triple time are charmingly tuneful. The next year, 1614, saw the publication of Barbarino's second book of solo motets, more interesting than the first, since he gives alternative simple and ornamented versions of the vocal part, explaining that some singers had found difficulty with the divisions of the 1610 volume. The simplified versions are for them, and also provide a basic outline for experienced singers to decorate; while the ornamented versions are addressed to singers of good technique who lack the ability to improvise embellishments. That these represent a tasteful transformation of the original melody can be seen from the beginning of the Eastertide motet *Haec dies* [Ex. 9]. The ornaments strengthen and diversify the melodic line, and are carefully matched to the mood of the text. Florid passagework is reserved for 4/4 time, lilting melismas and hemiolas for triple. The shifting modulations on the sharp side of F major at 'mori dignatus est' show a developing grasp of tonality. Barbarino's melodic

Ex.9. Barbarino, *Haec dies*

spontaneity is apparent in other motets, such as the *Salve Regina* [Ex. 10]. This is the solo motet at its best; it clearly influenced the Venetian composers of a decade later.

Other composers of solo motets in the second decade of the seventeenth

Ex.10. Barbarino, *Salve Regina*

century include Pietro Pace, and Alessandro Gualtieri, who demonstrated that the genre could succeed with the most restrained ornamentation when the voice part was melodious and the bass line varied. An especially talented minor figure who worked in comparative provincial obscurity in the Ferrara district was Biagio Tomasi; the doleful text of his *Versa est in luctum* of 1615 ('My lyre is turned to grief, my organ to the sound of weeping') was often set because of the opportunities it afforded for intense mood painting, here enhanced by the telling use of chromaticism. A striking feature in Ex. 11 is the boldly dissonant variant of the 7–6 progression in bars 39, 42, and 45 which, though here used in a monodic context, recalls the opening of Monteverdi's five-part madrigal *La piaga ch'ho nel core*[7] [Ex. 11].

Ex. 11. Tomasi, *Versa est in luctum*

On the whole, the solo, duet, and trio textures were considered best for motets. By far the greater proportion of psalm and Mass settings were for larger, more mixed, forces, and published separately in functional liturgical compilations, since the long, fixed texts of the Mass and psalms generally failed to offer an expressive scope consonant with the richly expressive potential of the more intimate textures. Attempts made by Viadana, Tiburzio Massaino, Antonio Gualtieri, and Banchieri to alternate plainsong with the new concertato style were soon abandoned. Compared to traditional polyphony, florid solo writing consorted uneasily with plainsong; the modern style was found to be more compatible with a slightly less traditional device, that of *falso bordone*, with simple recitation leading to an ornamental cadence figure.[8]

By the 1620s, the motet for two or three voices and continuo was tending in one or other of two directions: either towards melody for its own sake, with greater expression and little emphasis on design, or towards more balanced structure involving refrains, motto ideas, and ground basses. Giovanni Battista Crivelli's first book of motets of 1626 contains examples of both these approaches. Like Grandi, he worked at one of the Ferrarese confraternities, and his motet book was popular enough to run into three editions. What had been progressive a decade earlier was now the norm: the short snatches of triple time blossom into complete middle sections with chains of eight-bar phrases, and the overall form is ternary, two 4/4 sections on either side of a central triple-time episode. This is all illustrated by the attractive duet *Ut flos ut rosa*, whose musical interest is enhanced by the varied use of a pleasantly sequential Alleluia refrain, and the development of the opening music at the reprise.[9]

In the field of this expressive and declamatory style, Monteverdi naturally exerted a strong influence on composers working in Venice, like Giovanni Rovetta, who was a singer in the St. Mark's choir in the year when he published his Opus 1 (*Salmi concertati*, 1626). The melodies of his long, wayward duet *Salve Regina*, at the end of that volume, are closely modelled on Monteverdi's freely modulating operatic recitative, with leading-note to tonic slurs at cadences, and 'Scotch snap' rhythms. Grandi, who, as Monteverdi's assistant *maestro*, also worked in Venice until leaving for Bergamo in 1627, was mainly interested in monodies and the new genre of motets with obbligato instruments, but at the end of the decade (1630) he added his sixth and last concertato motet book to the series he had published between 1610 and 1619. By now his style relied much less on the imitative techniques of his early years; there were still Alleluia refrains, but triple time was slower and more *arioso*, with melodious quaver movement, while 4/4 time had the definite character of recitative over a slow-moving bass line.

The alternative to this generally free framework of duet and trio writing was the adoption of chaconne or ostinato techniques used in secular music. For the few composers of two- and three-part psalms and Masses, the problems posed by long texts were better solved by thematic organization than by free expression. Carlo Milanuzzi attempted in his *Concerto sacro* of 1627 to round psalm settings off by returning to the music for the opening verse at the 'Sicut erat', and perhaps also by alluding to it in the middle. This rondo idea is highly developed in the second *Lauda Jerusalem*, where the opening music and text recur several times,[10] and in the second *Beatus vir*, where the recurring material is actually built over a twice-repeated ground bass, with interludes in triple time; here the upper parts become more elaborate with each reprise of the bass.

Grandi, whose melodies were much more distinguished than Milanuzzi's, did not need to rely on such thematic organization to preserve the musical interest in his three-part *Messa e salmi* of 1630. His psalms are in sections – now an established practice – contrasting chordal and imitative writing, tutti and solo, triple and 4/4 time. The Credo of the Mass in particular is a superb instance of stylistic simplicity combined with unflagging melodic and harmonic interest, which culminate in the 'Et incarnatus' section; there are no stunted thematic ideas but continuously unfolding melody – a remarkable solution to the problems of the long, unwieldy Credo text [Ex. 12].

Solo motet writing in the 1620s became centred on Venice and the surrounding area, and it was then that Grandi, as vice-*maestro* at St. Mark's, and also as an active composer of secular monodies in the new *aria* style, made his contribution to this repertory, his most important collection being

Ex. 12. Grandi, *Messa a 3*

Ex. 12 (*cont.*)

the *Motetti a voce sola* (1621). Other solo motets were published in the volumes of works with obbligato violins that were also occupying Grandi at this time, and in anthologies like Simonetti's *Ghirlanda sacra* (1625). One of Grandi's four contributions to this last work was the exquisite *O quam tu pulchra es*, which captures the perfumed, erotic atmosphere of its Song of Songs text.[11] The opening motto idea is imaginatively integrated with the various recitative and aria-like elements, and is itself finally extended at 'veni coronaberis'. The anguish of love-sickness at the end is conveyed by a striking change of key from G minor to A minor and lastly by the unsettled II–I cadence in the bass – the 7–6 suspension is more tense than the 4–3, since it resolves not on to a major but a diminished triad. That Grandi had excellent singers available in Venice can be seen from the extraordinary range of the demanding bass solo *Salvum me fac Deus*, from his third book of motets with violins (1629), which, though published after he had left for Bergamo, could well have been written for the same bass as Monteverdi's equally difficult *Ab aeterno ordinata sum*. The text, the first three verses of Psalm 69, with its turbulent alternations of black despair and glimmering hope, was one that inspired several composers. Downward-sweeping melodic lines express the words 'infixus sum in limo profundi'. After a turbulent 'storm' episode, the psalmist's voice dries up ('raucae factae sunt') in a dark, distant E minor, entering again with a descending chromatic tetrachord (bar 102); but 'dum spero', at first a hopeless, falling phrase (bar 107), later gains increasing confidence as the fourths rise in sequence, leading to a flood of ornamentation at the close [Ex. 13].

Ghirlanda sacra, besides including four solo motets apiece by Grandi and Monteverdi, is representative of the work of lesser composers working in the Veneto, many of whom had considerable talent. They used the typical devices of monody – transpositions, sequences, repeated notes, chromaticism, and surprising modulations to vary the vocal line. They contrasted long, slow phrases with brilliant semiquaver divisions for expressive purposes, but acknowledged the growing use of ostinato by employing plodding, sequential bass figures derived from the fashionable secular aria. The influence of the aria led to the emancipation of a melodious style of triple-time writing; pieces would actually begin in this measure, with the contrasted, ornate 4/4 style coming later, as in solo motets by Leandro Gallerano, Girolamo Casati, and Orazio Tarditi. Some pieces in Tarditi's *Celesti fiori* of 1629 begin on a long-held note or a series of repeated notes, in the manner of oratorio recitative; his motet *Transfige dulcissime Jesu* is an example of a true monody which lacks any overall musical form and is inspired by the text alone – a type fairly rare in sacred music. A further important collection of 1629 was Francesco Turini's book of solo motets. Turini was also active in the field of secular and instrumental music, and his other church music was generally conservative. In the preface, he explains that the motets are written in the alto clef so that boy singers may be able to practise in that clef; for men singers a different part, which doubles the continuo line, is also given for each piece. In the less emotional motets, the interplay between continuo and voice, whereby an idea is stated by the former and taken up by the latter in quasi-imitation, represents a technique initiated by Viadana and by now entirely conventional in solo motets. More ornamental vocal writing presupposes a more static, independent continuo,

Ex.13. Grandi, *Salvum me fac Deus*

as in this excerpt from *Venite gentes* [Ex. 14]. Here the elaborate ornamental writing, with its freely constructed roulades, is quite Monteverdian. But this is quite rare in the work of provincial composers, who in the 1620s were more intent on expanding the restrained, controlled art of melody, and indeed all that was 'artificial' in the best sense of the word.

The plague that swept northern Italy in 1630 seems to have paralysed music publishing in Milan and Venice for at least the next five years. It is symptomatic that in a field (instrumental music) which has been completely catalogued,[12] we find, in the five years from 1626 to 1630, thirty-two publications listed from these two cities, but a remarkable drop to only seven in the following five years from 1631 to 1635. From 1636 to 1640, the number had risen again to the more normal level of twenty-two. One of the

Ex. 14. Turini, *Venite gentes*

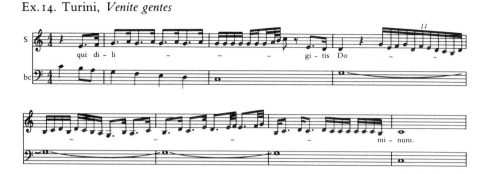

publications from the lean period, Giovanni Rovetta's *Motetti concertati* of 1635, contains duet and trio motets that show a penchant for some kind of organized musical form, often of the refrain variety. A rare hymn setting (*Ave maris stella*) has the same bass line for three verses, but varied parts for the three voices; the verses are to alternate, says Rovetta in a rubric in the score, with organ music – an organ hymn setting of the appropriate chant, perhaps.

For other composers, expressiveness was of more importance than thematic design, though the overall ternary shape was in widespread use. Alberto Lazari wrote good extended melodies in his *Armonie spirituali* of 1637; ornaments, however elaborate, form an indispensable part of the tune, and triple-time passages continue the rounded melodies in the manner of an *arioso* with sedate tempo. An extract from the duet *In sanctitate fulgida* also illustrates the use of long tail-melismas on 'jubila' [Ex. 15].

In the duets from Orazio Tarditi's fourth book of motets (1637), the use of both singers is reserved for the last bars of each line of text by way of climax; Tarditi was a capable melodist, not in need of ornament to bolster up his tunes. This tendency to concentrate on monodic writing for individual voices in turn represents the other side of the coin from the contrapuntal interplay favoured in earlier years, and was especially relevant to dialogue motets like *Heu dolor* from Nicolò Fontei's *Melodiae sacrae* of 1638, an impressive collection dedicated to the Holy Roman Emperor. This is a dialogue between the troubled soul and God, who changes the mood from unease to hope, particularly by breaking into a *concitato* style as He encourages the soul to 'fight and conquer'; at the end the voices combine to sing a 'chorus' of moral comment. Dialogues also appear in Gasparo Casati's third book of *Sacri concenti* (1644), one being between the devil, an angel, and a man. This type of music was almost certainly used for spiritual recreation rather than in liturgical contexts.

A few composers of duets and trios were feeling their way towards organization of the music by means of repeated bass figures. Carlo Milanuzzi continued to do so in his *Hortus sacer deliciarum* of 1636, building

Ex.15. Lazari, *In sanctitate fulgida*

up his music on 'walking' bass lines with continuous crotchet movement made up of cadence notes (for example B C D G). When repeated often enough – even in different keys – such basses become a kind of ground. They were the antithesis of the slow continuo line that supported recitative, and were in some ways less suited to the thinner scorings than to large-scale works, where much more varied music could be built above them than was possible with just two or three voices. However, Tarquinio Merula's ground bass psalm *Beatus vir* (*Pegaso musicale*, 1640) succeeds because the bass theme, the *Romanesca*, is much slowed down and spread over twelve bars.

In small-scale music, the ground bass principle worked best when it was reserved for individual sections, to be contrasted with freer writing, as in Gasparo Casati's *Alleluia jubilat ecclesia*, from his first book of concertato motets of 1643, where a popular, jerky chaconne idea (best known for its use in Monteverdi's duet *Zefiro torna*) is used for an Alleluia refrain. Another frequently-used bass figure, the descending four notes from tonic to dominant, appears in Giovanni Antonio Rigatti's excellent duet *Salve Regina,* appended to his *Messa e salmi ariosi* (reprinted 1643), which exemplifies the work of the talented post-plague generation working in the Veneto during Monteverdi's last years. Headed 'adagio et affettuoso più che si può', this is an emotionally highly charged work, frequently changing to triple time and back. The descending four-note bass is used in the minor key, and also modulates [Ex. 16a]. The music displays a melodic exuberance, and a contrapuntal tension, found in the very best duets of the day, sacred or secular – in particular we find such devices as false relations (bars 22, 34), falling sevenths (bars 42–3), and powerful dissonance caused by the use of static melody and moving bass line (bars 44–7). There is also an

Ex.16(a). Rigatti, *Salve Regina*

Ex. 16 (*cont.*)

extravagantly expressive and protracted setting of the words 'o dulcis virgo
Maria' towards the end [Ex. 16b]. Perhaps this lurching *rubato*, coupled with
the written-in tempo changes, is overdone, but the passage is undoubtedly a
noteworthy document of the development of musical expressiveness.[13]

Ex. 16(b). Rigatti, *Salve Regina*

Like the duet and trio, the solo motet continued to develop after the
plague years. One of the most instructive publications was Ignazio Donati's
second book of solo motets (1636) – a didactic work concerned with certain
aspects of vocal technique. It is worth reproducing the preface in full for
what it tells us of early baroque singing practice:[14]

I have composed these few *concerti*, with ornamentation added, for the training of boys, girls, or nuns, and for those who do not possess a singing voice.

(1) The boy must be taught to sing with full and vigorous voice till the melodies and their variations in the pieces below are committed to memory. At first he should not sing too fast, but repeat the notes gradually increasing the tempo so as to attain the habit of singing them all in one breath, until he has memorized the tune.

(2) When the boy can sing the notes well, he should then be taught vowel sounds or syllables with A, E, and O, the customary way to shape the gullet; he should attack and release each note well, uttering a certain quantity of each vowel with the same voice and breathing throughout. Though at first it may appear unsuitable to utter A, E, and O, adjustment can nevertheless be made to the voice production to avoid too vigorous an attack; but the vocal attack must be made both incisively and in a relaxed manner.

(3) The head should be held high and the eyes should look up, the mouth should be half open so as not to lose too much breath, the neck should be straight, the lips still, and the face should avoid contorted expressions. The true point of vocal attack is at the larynx.

(4) I have barred the voice part so that anyone who wishes to sing in strict time may be aware of the beat.

(5) In this kind of solo *cantilena* one should never count out each beat, but merely apply oneself to singing with a deliberately broad measure, making expression with exclamations, loudening and softening the tone as well as one is able, and with *sforzandi* at times; one should not sing with nervousness or fear. From his part the organist can see all the singer is doing, and he will always make allowances with his playing, even if he should wish to add further ornaments. But patience is needed.

The motets themselves represent a cross-section of the monodic art, some in the anguished style of Monteverdi's and Grandi's best pieces, employing a great freedom of harmony and modulation, others more melodious with the typical ternary shape.

This sectional form is found in many solo motets after 1635, including those by Giovanni Battista Chinelli (first book of solo motets, 1637) and Cherubino Busatti (*Compago*, 1640); examples from each of these collections will show up vividly contrasted approaches to sacred monody around 1640. Chinelli's *O Maria felix* is written in the most ornate declamatory idiom, and even in the triple-time section considerable vocal acrobatics are required for the execution of rapid changes of dynamic and sighing effects [Ex. 17]. Chinelli introduces occasional solos for the continuo, to give the voice time to recover from such extravagant roulades. The final section finishes quite abruptly in keeping with the sense of the words, 'behold I die'; the frankly amorous nature of such music is common in Marian motets. A very talented singer would be needed for this motet – not so for Busatti's *Quid video*, the gorgeous simplicity of whose melodies is quite original. Though this piece is headed 'for Pentecost', its text is not liturgical, but a meditation, couched in a personal vein, on the descent of the Holy Spirit. Busatti has no need of virtuosity to bolster up his music, and relies very little on semiquaver runs in

Ex.17. Chinelli, *O Maria felix*

4/4 time. He prefers short, regular, and balanced phrases occasionally enlivened by chromaticism or word painting [Ex. 18]. His triple-time writing can also be most attractive, as in the continuous melodic outpouring that forms the central *arioso* of *Quid video*.

The musical evidence suggests that vocal display could all too often oust simple melodic charm. Sometimes, of course, this was entirely relevant to the text, as in Rigatti's aggressive and virtuoso alto solo *Congregati sunt inimici nostri* (printed in 1647), whose battle-like fanfare motives, rapid tonic-dominant chord changes, and repeated semiquavers in the continuo cannot fail to have been influenced by Monteverdi's *Combattimento di Tancredi e Clorinda*. Melodic charm tended to be proportionate to the amount of triple time in a work. In another alto solo, Gasparo Casati's *Fuge, fuge* (1643), this metre dwarfs the short and recitative-like twenty-eight bars of 4/4 that form the contrasted central section. The two most common ground basses mentioned above make an appearance, though Casati cleverly extends the four-note figure to give a full twenty-three bars of continuously descending bass line, one note per bar, and then twelve bars of ascending movement to lead to the final cadence; these wide spans in the continuo aptly convey the 'flying' idea of which the voice is singing. A rigid ground bass treatment would have been not merely inappropriate but would have contradicted the words, and in any case its use was rare in the

Ex.18. Busatti, *Quid video*

solo motet. That this should be so may seem odd by comparison with its popularity among composers of the secular aria, until we remember that, whereas the aria texts were strophic and therefore suited to vocal variations over a fixed bass, hardly any sacred texts consisted of anything but prose.

Equally, even though 4/4 and triple time in the solo motet could often assume the character of operatic recitative and aria respectively, the parallel cannot be pushed too far. The musical priorities of church music and opera were different. In opera, aria had greater musical potentialities than recitative, which acted as a musical prop for dramatic dialogue. The best sacred monodies, on the other hand, were those of the declamatory type, which combined the spontaneity of the best recitative with the mood-expression of the aria. The more melodious style was in some ways less personal, more artificial. The spread of triple time around 1640 was a measure of the increasing influence of the operatic *bel canto*, in the face of which the declamatory approach gave way. The close contact with the words that it inspired was in some measure lost until the spirit of Pietism inspired Germans of the later baroque era to infuse fervour anew into the solo cantata.

The motet with obbligato instruments

By the early years of the seventeenth century, churches had for some time been giving employment to a small number of instrumental players as well as singers. Their function had been to support the voices and provide instrumental music, but now, with the concertato style gaining hold, composers began to integrate instruments and voices in the same texture. At first the most common procedure was to replace lower voices in four- and five-part motets with specified instruments, as Viadana did in his *Repleatur* for AT and two trombones (*Cento concerti III*, 1609). Arcangelo Crotti and Leone Leoni did the same, but their instrumental lines were in no way distinct in style from the vocal ones, and were, indeed, optional, while other composers, like Caterina Assandra and Arcangelo Borsaro, used a kind of reduced *cori spezzati* technique with pairs of unequal voices and instruments (e.g. SB, violin, and *violone*) in dialogue, but still without idiomatic contrast. A texture derived from polychoral music, where it was often used to make a 'coro grave' whether instruments were specified or not, was the solo or duet with three or four trombones, a rich sonority in which the trombone writing came to take on the character of sustained accompaniment quite distinct from the more agile vocal style. Amante Franzoni and Borsaro both wrote for voice and four instruments, but a particularly impressive use of the texture is Ercole Porta's *Corda Deo dabimus* for SA and three trombones (*Sacro convito*, 1620). Even here the latter are optional, but they add a remarkable depth of colour; in other places, the duet writing is brilliantly contrapuntal. We might coin the phrase 'trombone motet' to label this kind of piece; the genre culminates in a work like *Absalom fili mi* from Schütz's *Symphoniae sacrae* of 1629, which must hark back to the 'coro grave' scoring of polychoral motets by his teacher, Gabrieli.

Such sonorities as these were not perhaps particularly novel, but the brilliant and idiomatic use of pairs of obbligato upper instruments (violins, cornetts, and so on) which Monteverdi transferred from *Orfeo* to the large Magnificat of the 1610 Vespers undoubtedly was. Hardly exploiting the tutti at all, he combined these high instruments with voices in a way that foreshadowed the few-voiced motet with instrumental obbligati, and it is strange that once he left Mantua he never returned to this unbridled style. The talent available to him at Mantua was exceptional, however, and less fortunate composers were contenting themselves with little *sinfonie* for a pair of violins and perhaps a *chitarrone* or a bass melody-instrument to lend some unity to a motet, as in Grandi's *Factum est silentium*, appended to his fourth motet book (1616). Scored for four voices, two violins, and *chitarrone* (an instrument seldom specified in part-books), this motet may well have been intended for solemn performance on St. Michael's Day, to whose liturgy the text belongs; instruments would provide a festive addition to the few voices of the everyday concertato texture.

It was during the 1620s that Grandi turned away from the ordinary concertato motet towards this new and exciting genre of 'motetti con sinfonie di violini', publishing three pioneering volumes. For he was now assistant *maestro* at St. Mark's, and had at his disposal not only fine singers (for whom the solo motets discussed earlier were written), but also excellent instrumental players. Monteverdi, who as *maestro* seems to have been responsible for large-scale music on great feasts, hardly showed any interest in exploiting this new medium for sacred purposes (apart from the four tautly-constructed, strophic Vesper hymns with violin ritornellos in the *Selva morale*).[15] Certainly, it was suited to the smaller motets used at weekday Masses, and would have contrasted well with the *stile antico* settings of the Ordinary that were the ferial fare at St. Mark's. Equally, it was the kind of medium appropriate for spiritual recreation in a domestic setting, since many of the texts Grandi set were not strictly liturgical and, when selected from the Song of Songs, might well be madrigalian in feeling; the indication 'per cantar et sonar col chitarrone' also suggests its suitability for rooms without an organ.

O vos omnes is a fine example of a piece where the instruments – in this case three viols, a texture which underscores the doleful mood in a setting of a free paraphrase of the Good Friday Reproaches – do nothing but play a sorrowful chromatic *sinfonia* from time to time (in most of the pieces in the *Motetti con sinfonie I* (1621) the instruments are largely limited to this unifying role). The soprano solo passages are set in a recitative-like style, conveying the words with simplicity and clarity, in a manner more akin to chanting than to operatic recitative. These 'chanted' solos, setting the various Reproaches, lead into the anguished 'attendite' refrain, which contains one of Grandi's most gorgeous melodic climaxes. The reiterated A minor of the former and the daring E minor of the latter have the effect of emphasizing the grief of the final D minor, lower and flatter in key [Ex. 19].

Ex.19(a & b). Grandi, *O vos omnes*

Ex. 19(b)

In other motets the instruments take a much greater part in the musical argument; this participation, coupled with Grandi's increasing predilection for subtle variation techniques, makes for some excellently taut musical structures. *Bone Jesu verbum Patris* (1621) is one of the most satisfying of these, scored for equal pairs of voices and violins with continuo – a new-look *cori spezzati* procedure, yet delightfully intimate in texture and colour. The text is a conventional enough hymn of praise, though the description of the 'blessed city' in the middle section contains some interesting plays on words (e.g. 'ubi est secura aeternitas, et aeterna tranquillitas, et tranquilla felicitas . . .'). The form of the motet is ternary, each section opening with the obviously inter-related *sinfonia* and 'Bone Jesu' themes [Ex. 20a] (bars 1 and 14): The middle section is distinguished by its much less active, recitative-like bass line. The ample variety in the thirteen bars of the opening *sinfonia* owes much to unpredictable phrase-lengths, a feature that enables Grandi to compress it to only eight bars on its second appearance at bar 43 [Ex. 20b]; precisely the same happens to the opening vocal section (bars 14–24), shortened to only four-and-a-half bars (bars 51–5). This suggests the hand of a composer who took meticulous care to avoid the predictable, and tempered an intellectual conception with the spontaneity of his most expressive music. Schütz must have admired a motet like this, for the *Symphoniae sacrae I*, the fruit of his second Venetian visit in 1629, share the scoring and approach of many of Grandi's 'motetti con sinfonie'. Indeed, he later parodied Grandi's *Lilia convallium* (second book, *c.* 1622), a motet which plays off three equal pairs of sopranos, tenors, and violins in the manner of another of Schütz's Italian idols, Monteverdi.[16]

Ex.20(a). Grandi, *Bone Jesu verbum Patris*

Ex. 20(a) *(cont.)*

Ex. 20(b). Grandi, *Bone Jesu verbum Patris*

Schütz followed German fashion in introducing more varied instrumental obbligati into his motets; Grandi stuck mainly to two violins, though he added a bassoon in one piece and in another wrote for violin and trombone, an unequal pair that matched the vocal grouping of soprano and tenor. This latter setting was *O beate Benedicte* from the *Motetti con sinfonie III*, published in 1629 after Grandi had moved to Bergamo. The motet may well have been intended for S. Maria Maggiore, whose choir included players of these two instruments; if so, they must have been most proficient, judging from the demands of the brilliant opening *sinfonia*. In some of the works of this collection we can see the influence of the strophic secular aria that had also engaged Grandi's attention in the 1620s; its style is, of course, ideal for a hymn setting like *Ave maris stella*, but it is perhaps most felicitously employed in *Amo Christum*, whose text, based on a responsory for St. Agnes' Day, is addressed to Christ by a virgin or female saint. The 'walking' bass of the secular aria underpins a violin ritornello and a brief vocal melody, both of which are progressively elaborated in distinct but entirely idiomatic styles.[17] In other motets the 'walking' crotchet bass of the aria is organized into an ostinato, over which the voice and violins alternate and vary their material, or a motto idea may be used for unification instead of a violin ritornello, as in *O beate Benedicte*, mentioned above. Altogether, by introducing an emphasis on structural experiments and delicate contrasts of vocal and instrumental colour without impairing the intimacy of the solo or duet motet, Grandi's 'motetti con sinfonie' show that he was capable of intellectual rigour as well as emotional expression; historically, they represent a fusion of monody and trio sonata that looked ahead to the mature baroque cantata style which spread to many other countries.

Most composers in the 1620s only wrote isolated motets for this medium. Among them were Leandro Gallerano, Giovanni Battista Aloisi, Antonio Gualtieri, Tarquinio Merula, and Giovanni Rovetta, several of whom added a bass melody-instrument, trombone or *violone*, to the violin passages: this suggests that there was no tradition of doubling the continuo line with a melody instrument throughout a piece, as became later baroque practice. After the plague of 1630, however, choirs were often pared down to a few solo singers and some string players (with the increasing domination of the violin), and the voices-and-violins scoring became more widely favoured, especially for psalm settings. Genuinely idiomatic writing for violins was taken for granted, and the violin parts themselves became more independent of each other, indulging in contrapuntal interplay with the voice as well as providing ritornellos. After 1635, composers who included a quantity of pieces with obbligati in their motet collections were Giovanni Bonachelli, Paolo Cornetti, Orazio Tarditi and Francesco Maria Marini, who again tended to add a special continuo part – for *violone*, bassoon, or *chitarrone* – to the violins; or else they tried more unusual scorings, such as the viol quartet of Marini's passionate alto solo *Jesu dulcis memoria* (*Concerti spirituali*, 1637). Their interludes consist of contrasted material, not a recurrent *sinfonia*, and they are also pitted against the voice in imaginative dialogue in masterly fashion as at the moment of relaxation, from the hectic 'et triunfator' to the beautifully delicate 'dulcedo ineffabilis' [Ex. 21]. The same procedure is

Ex.21. F. M. Marini, *Jesu dulcis memoria*

followed in *Omnes gentes* in which Marini sets a text in celebration of S. Marino, patron of the eponymous Republic, where he worked. Here he integrates the two duet textures (sopranos and violins) in an extended form consisting of close-knit sections punctuated by a clear (if simple) modulation scheme. Well-defined key schemes are found in similar works by Cornetti, and mark the progress of the baroque style; on the other hand, there was no noticeable increase in taut ground bass structures, which for this medium proved more useful in long psalms than in motets.

༄༅༔

CHAPTER VI

Small-scale Church Music (II)

The concertato motet in four, five, and six parts

WHEREAS the continuo was indispensable in works for the innovatory solo, duet, and trio textures, there seems to have been some uncertainty among Viadana's immediate followers at the beginning of the seventeenth century as to what its role might be in motets for the larger, more conventional, forces. One approach, in the face of the stylistic confusion of the day, was to publish compilations designed to be as widely useful as possible, as Giacomo Moro (from the town of Viadana, like Viadana himself) did in his *Concerti ecclesiastici* of 1604, which includes everything from solos to double-choir music. A more orderly scheme was devised by Adriano Banchieri in his *Ecclesiastiche sinfonie* of 1607, a collection of four-part motets divided under two headings – *sinfonia* and *concerto* – according to whether the bass was *seguente* or independent. Like the cautious theorist that he is, Banchieri shuns the term 'continuo' in his preface (he calls it the *basso seguente*), yet advises the player to study Agazzari's important treatise *Del sonare sopra il basso*, which appeared in the same year. The *sinfonie* are in a conservative vein similar to that of Viadana's least adventurous four-part works, sometimes self-consciously modal and sometimes exploiting academic contrapuntal procedures like inversion. Much more significant are the *concerti* which, by including an early example of the dialogue motet, remind us that Banchieri was an admired writer of madrigal comedies. In *Mulier cur plorans*, Mary Magdalen is conversing with Christ after the Resurrection. She is represented by three voices; single characters were often represented by multiple voices in the madrigal, and the practice persists in Schütz's *Resurrection History* of 1623. There is some attempt to evolve an interesting solo vocal line for Christ, and to illustrate Mary's surprise on recognizing him by syncopated, faltering chords [Ex. 22]. Other composers who adopted a rather ambivalent attitude to the continuo around 1610 were Giovanni Paolo Cima and Giovanni Ghizzolo, who wrote organ parts in score; they both worked at Milan and their style was still somewhat retrospective.[1] The motets of many composers were similar to Viadana's – simple and often chordal, though perhaps with more variety of rhythm.

Grandi also dominated the four- to six-part motet in the decade 1610–20. Whereas in solo, duet, and trio writing we saw that melody was important,

Ex. 22. Banchieri, *Mulier cur plorans*

here we find many examples of what might be termed the 'textural' motet, in which the interest is not in melodic lines but in a constantly varying 'terraced' approach to texture. One such setting is the fine five-part *Versa est in luctum* (*Motetti a cinque voci*, 1614), whose text differs from the Viadana and Tomasi settings with the same title; the mood of gloom continues right through till the final ray of hope, and provides many opportunities for powerful expressiveness. This is achieved not by melodic elaboration but by fluid, syncopated rhythms and, in the widely modulating central section (heralded by an astonishing change of key at bar 36), anguished chromaticism and seventh harmonies [Ex. 23]. The tutti passages are not chordal, but made up of independent lines: the few chordal phrases are given to small groups (e.g. bars 25–6, 28–9). *Exaudi Deus*, another motet from the same collection, is thinner in texture.[2] It falls loosely into two sections each ending with the 'intende mihi' motif, in the supertonic at bar 61, and in the tonic at the end: this leaning on the supertonic abounds in early Grandi and is characteristic of the transition from modality to functional tonality. In the first section, each line of text is set to contrasted ideas worked out together in a variety of combinations, for example, the slow notes of 'Exaudi' and the crotchets of 'orationem', or the rounded phrase 'et ne despexeris' (bar 34) and the flurry of quavers at 'deprecationem'. The second half, on the other

Ex. 23. Grandi, *Versa est in luctum*

Ex.23 (*cont.*)

hand, contains extended, sequential development of themes, one of which (bar 82) is chromatic, and similar to that in the central section of *Versa est in luctum*. Other motets have a more rigid approach to texture, playing off tuttis against extended passages for duet or trio groupings. One piece from Grandi's third book of motets (also 1614), *O intemerata*, is scored for an unusual SSBB grouping, but this is in effect a reduced *cori spezzati* work for two SB groups; with the lighter scoring, Grandi can exploit the melodic potential of well-contrasted solo voices, adding ornaments towards the end.

    Grandi was quick to see that the dialogue rather than the 'textural' motet afforded his melodic imagination fuller rein. Although there were, as we have seen, dialogues of a more intimate kind for duet and trio, the larger texture allowed exchanges between solo voices and groups in a dramatic fashion; the group (often of three voices) might represent a crowd of onlookers, or provide a commentary. *Veniat dilectus meus*, from Grandi's fifth book of motets (1619), is a dialogue motet on a Song of Songs text very similar to *Surge propera* discussed earlier.[3] The first part is a conversation between husband and wife with extended melodies, ending at 'surgamus'; the 'videamus' passage (bar 54) is in effect a short coda. The tenor duet (bars 78–89) is like a commentary on the scene, to which the soprano replies, and from bar 76 the material of bars 52–62 is developed in four parts: it was quite customary to end the dialogue with all the voices in ensemble fashion. *Plorabo die ac nocte* (fourth book of motets, 1616) is at once one of the best examples of Grandi's mature melodic writing and of his copious fund of tragic expression:[4] it has dialogue elements, but is essentially an impassioned lament of the Madonna, who is personified by the soprano only at the end. The music unfolds through beautiful solos – rich in sequences, diminished fourths, chromatic inflections, and the like – for each of the four voices in turn, summed up by short, tense polyphonic strains from time to time (these are cleverly interlinked). The true dialogue technique appears at 'et sciant omnes populi' (bar 55), where the lower voices represent mourners in dialogue with Mary; in a remarkable ending, her last notes tail off into sobs.

The idea of alternating distinct solos (or duets) with a recurring tutti was the essence of a third form of motet, the *cantilena*. We have seen how Viadana used this technique in his four-part *Dic Maria*; Croce worked it out more fully in his *Sacre cantilene* of 1610.[5] Grandi adopted the label for some of his 1619 motets, in particular *Diem festum*, where only two tenors have a solo role; their parts have a much more idiomatic style than Croce's, and proceed over a slow bass line.

All three types of motet, the 'textural', dialogue, and *cantilena*, were adopted by Grandi's contemporaries during the decade 1610–20. Evidently the dialogue type was thought particularly appropriate for certain biblical texts; Giovanni Battista Fergusio's *Gloria in altissimis* (*Motetti e dialoghi*, 1612) is a seven-part dialogue between shepherds and angels, each represented by separated blocks of voices. The same idea inspired settings of the Christmas dialogue *Quem vidistis pastores* by Serafino Patta (*Sacrorum canticorum*, 1613) and Aurelio Signoretti (first book of motets, 1615). But whereas Patta simply makes the whole five-part chorus take up the shepherds' reply 'Natum vidimus', Signoretti devises a rounded *ABCB* form with an Alleluia refrain, and gives the shepherds' words a different setting on their second appearance. For composers blessed with a melodic gift, the solo-versus-group dialogue, common in Grandi, was a congenial proposition. An excellent example of this format, again based on the Christmas theme, is Ignazio Donati's *Transeamus usque ad Bethlehem*, one of two four-part dialogues in the *Concerti ecclesiastici a 1–4 voci* of 1618, in which the angel (soprano) announces the Nativity to the shepherds (three tenors, who sing solo as well as in ensemble) before a joint chorus 'exultemus . . . Alleluia'. Donati was an important contributor to the de-velopment of the Latin dialogue, writing a total of twelve in all.[6]

Composers also worked at the 'textural' type of motet. Often these lacked any particular formal design, being laid out as a series of linked paragraphs for every line of text, each consisting of small groupings which led by way of a 'textural crescendo' to a tutti. Giovanni Ceresini and Pietro Pace were among many to favour this scheme, which depends for its success upon the quality of the material being developed in each paragraph. Only Donati came consistently close to Grandi in producing such fine illustrations of this procedure as are found in the former's *Motetti in concerto* (1616) and *Motetti concertati* (1618). In the dramatic *Ecce confundentur*, from the latter collection, the text describes the fate of God's enemies, and later, the safety of his chosen ones. The music matches this with its initially unsettled tone. The opening phrases of the motet, over a chromatic bass, contain ideas that invite development and contrast[7] leading through sharp, changing harmo-nies at the words 'and his hurricane will scatter them' ('et turbo') to sure and confident homophony. The continuo provides a harmonic background to these events, moving much more slowly than the brisk, sequential basses of Donati's duet and trio motets. Although much of this music is contrapuntal, the vocal lines abound in imaginative melodic ideas. The five-part texture was favoured for this sort of motet; whether scored for SSATB or SATTB, it afforded the typical contrasts of more or less equal pairs of voices over the bass, which could lend adequate variety even to the shortest motet. The four-part motet tended to acquire more rounded, less clipped melodies, as in *Domine exaudi* from Salvatore Santa Maria's *Sacrorum concentuum* (1620), where the extended vocal lines, decorated by specified *trillo* ornaments, result at times in a curiously dissonant part writing [Ex. 24].

Massive six- and seven-part textures were still found in motets of 1618 by men with Venetian connections like Giovanni Battista Grillo and Giovanni Priuli, the latter of whom shows a characteristic Venetian preference for a rich, bottom-heavy sound with multiple tenor and bass parts. Priuli's impressive *Salvum me fac Deus* (*Sacrorum concentuum I*) recalls Gabrieli in many details: the anguished dissonances of 'infixus sum', the plunging phrases of 'in limo profundi' (bars 32–45) and the agitated, rapid rhythms of the central climax are all very much in the pre-concertato madrigal vein.[8]

Many composers apparently felt the need to introduce some structural coherence into their motets. This took the form of simple rondo and *cantilena* types or of shapes like *ABCCA* or *ABCDC*, the sections being distinguished by scoring and/or metre. In this regard, the developments of the 1620s are illustrated not by Grandi, who had by then turned his attention to the motet with instruments, but by Giovanni Battista Crivelli and Tarquinio Merula. Crivelli's charming *O Maria mater gratiae* (first book of motets, 1626) falls into two halves, respectively unified by the opening motif in thirds and the phrase for 'ave felix': the first half is punctuated by

Ex.24. Santa Maria, *Domine exaudi*

two sonorous tutti cadences, whereas the second moves steadily towards a climax whose contrapuntal working involves the inversion of the 'ave felix' idea.[9] Merula's *Concerti spirituali* of 1628 contains a motet intended (as its title implies) for dedication-days, the four-part *In dedicatione templi*, whose *AABBC* plan, with exact repeats, runs to the typical 100-bar length, and, thanks to Merula's economy with thematic material, forms a coherent whole.[10]

Grandi returned to the concertato motet in his sixth book of 1630: an example is *O porta caeli* in refrain form; setting a metrical text, the refrain makes delightfully unconventional use of the hemiola rhythm in triple time, and acts as a foil to the elaborate 4/4 episodes, which express the changing moods of the text as Mary is likened variously to the 'star of the sea' and 'terror of demons'.[11] The identical 'Virgo Maria' cadences before the refrain at bars 59–61 and 82–4, and the chaconne-like opening of the motet, are also worth noting. Yet another Marian motet, *Quae est ista*, revives the dialogue, this time between a questioning human and an answering angel: 'Who is this ascending over the desert as a plume of smoke?' 'This is Mary, who is entering Heaven.'[12] In both these motets triple time is now emancipated, dominating the rhythmic idiom and boasting rounded melodies in its own right.

After the interruption caused by the plague of 1630, it seemed that on the whole the four- to six-part motet without obbligato instruments was becoming obsolete – composers either included instruments or wrote for the duet or trio texture. Those who still wrote motets of this type (e.g. Rovetta, Rigatti, and Merula) showed a preference for some kind of formal organization. Exceptions to this were the few straightforward textural motets by composers such as Giovanni Battista Aloisi and Francesco Milani. The exquisite five-part *Ave verum* from the latter's *Letanie e motetti* (1638) has conventional contrasts of voice-pairs (emphasized by the SSTTB scoring) and solid, but no less expressive tutti writing with dissonant passing notes.[13] In conclusion, we may mention another four-part motet, a setting of the Marian antiphon *Salve Regina* from Giovanni Bonachelli's *Corona di sacri gigli* of 1642. Clearly, even at this date, the contrapuntal motet with expressive melodic strands over a slow bass was still a reality. The most subtle aspect of the motet is its unification by the constant recurrence of the 'Regina mater misericordiae' phrase from the opening exposition (Ex. 25a), in adroit contrapuntal combinations with later material, e.g. 'ad te' (Ex. 25b) or 'et Jesum' (Ex. 25c) [Ex. 25]. The very continuity of the musical

Ex.25(a, b, & c). Bonachelli, *Salve Regina*

Ex. 25(b)

Ex. 25(c)

argument is in sharp contrast to sectionalized, refrain motets. Characteristic of the 1640s is the bass voice's high degree of independence from the continuo, the greater emphasis than before on the dominant for structural cadences, and the adventurous approach to tonality (the cadence at 'exules filiae Evae' in Ex. 25b appears a few bars later in the submediant of G minor, E flat).

The 'textural' motet dominated the four- to six-part repertory in the early decades of the seventeenth century; some composers had turned to the dialogue (often using contrasted groups rather than individual voices), whose expressive needs demanded the melodic gift of such masters as Grandi and Donati. The 'textural' type, whether formally organized or based on a free succession of distinctive ideas, proved attractive to many composers. It was in the realm of the psalm setting that formal problems loomed larger.

The concertato psalm setting

The Vesper psalm setting was, as we saw earlier, a comparatively recent phenomenon in the history of church music, appearing around 1570 and soon spreading throughout northern Italy. The decline of plainsong, which the Council of Trent hardly succeeding in arresting, was partly responsible for the growth of harmonized psalm settings;[14] indeed, the Council gave a new lease of life to a 'purified' polyphonic style, which was rapidly adopted for the psalms prescribed for Vespers – after Mass, the most important service in many churches. The most common technique was the *alternatim*, plainsong alternating with polyphony, which was also applied to the hymn and Magnificat. This ensured musical contrast and kept the setting to a reasonable duration since the plainsong verses were short, an important consideration in music for regular liturgical use. In this context, through-composed works like Lassus' *Penitential psalms*, in polyphony throughout though with varied textures, stood apart as more personal art-music. Another more up-to-date technique was that of *falso bordone*, in which repeated chords in free rhythm led to a melismatic cadence phrase at the end of each half-verse. This also alternated with plainsong, but it was uncomplicated and highly adaptable, and was a repeated feature of psalm collections from 1575 to about 1610, after which it died out.[15] We have already seen how some composers tried to adapt it to the new monodic style (cf. pp. 69–70).

With the development of the small-scale concertato style at the turn of the century, the composer of psalm settings faced a problem. The texts of the most frequently-occurring psalms and also the Magnificat were somewhat neutral in their imagery, and, while ideally suited to an emotionally detached contrapuntal or homophonic treatment, did not afford scope for the word painting and affective writing possible in the new style.[16] Moreover the texts were long, making musical coherence difficult to achieve in a through-composed setting (most rejected the *alternatim* scheme on the grounds that the concertato idiom was incompatible with plainsong); since the concertato style depended much on the repetition and development of musical ideas, a continuous setting would be in danger of becoming excessively long – perhaps three or four times as long as a motet. Thus the concertato psalm took far longer than the motet to become established; indeed, many lesser composers declined to face these issues, adhering to the late sixteenth-century idiom for their Vespers music and nailing their colours firmly to the *stile antico* mast. Clearly, the increasing number of compilations of Office music in this traditional idiom issued by the Venetian publishers was intended for ordinary Sundays and lesser feasts; for great occasions, large-scale works, possibly with instruments, would have been the order of the day.

The only man to reject the prevailing unadventurous spirit was Monteverdi, whose *Laetatus sum* and smaller Magnificat from the Vespers of 1610 merit discussion at this point.[17] They were remarkable experimental works in the new vein, combining (as do the larger psalms) a cantus firmus presentation of the old plainsong tone with the bustling concertato style and its 'walking' bass lines, varied rhythms, dialogue, and echo devices; the slight modality of the G minor-major in the *Laetatus sum* and the isolated *falso bordone* verse near the end were by then a little old-fashioned. The music is highly individual, illustrating a struggle of styles rather than lapsing into the stylistic complacency of many minor composers.

Others gingerly followed suit in trying to marry the new style with the psalm setting. The reduction in size of many north Italian choirs ruled out the *cori spezzati* psalm setting and forced composers to accept that the 'neutral' *stile antico* was retrospective and often impracticable. A quasi-sectional form (each verse running on into the next with perhaps a pause before the doxology), and an average concertato texture of say, four parts, allowing some of the necessary contrasts (as in the 'textural' motet), seemed feasible — even if the length and neutrality of the texts still presented difficulties. Stefano Bernardi's *Psalmi integri* of 1613 were particularly successful, running into five editions; short solos and duets with pleasant melodies were contrasted with the tutti. Few others attempted this solution until towards 1620; Giacomo Finetti, Giovanni Cavaccio and Giovanni Paolo Nodari are among those who did, but the results were on the whole undistinguished. Antonio Burlini actually added optional instrumental parts for one high and one low instrument in his 1613 collection, but they tended to function as a substitute high voice and a continuo melody instrument respectively, hardly adding any new dimension to the musical effect. Francesco Bellazzi's *Salmi concertati* of 1624 were in true concertato idiom, but they demonstrate the psalm composer's difficulties; the texts were prescribed by the liturgy, and he had to work through a long psalm, little of which might call for expressive treatment. Thus, in *In te Domine speravi*, there is no call for solo melody, and the only unexpected event is the change to triple time at the doxology. Compared with this, a motet composer like Donati (who, as we have seen, set the first three verses of this psalm as an excellent little duet) had considerable freedom; he was able to choose the part of the psalm text that interested him, develop his musical ideas at leisure, and, within the expressive duet medium, dwell on the meaning of the words. There are, of course, opportunities for word painting in some psalm texts, and in the Magnificat, as at 'dispersit superbos. . . . exaltavit humiles', and we can find a robust, urgent response to these words in Amadio Freddi's setting (*Psalmi integri*, 1626); but there are few solo passages here, for the text seldom suggests them [Ex. 26].

It took a talented melodist like Ignazio Donati, who appended some psalms to his *Motetti concertati* of 1618, to avoid lapsing into this mainly

Ex.26. Freddi, Magnificat

Ex.27. Donati, *Confitebor*

nondescript approach to psalm settings. The six-part *Confitebor* is a textural work *par excellence*, presenting in turn fine, well-wrought solo melodies, imitations and counterpoints, and varied tuttis. Donati has a penchant for using sequential repetition and imitation to develop his ideas [Ex. 27]. A short, but arresting change to triple time heralds the doxology and rapidly modulates from F to D major, only to be abruptly contradicted by an immediate return to F at 'Sicut erat': harmony and modulation, as well as melody, contribute to the musical interest. The psalms of Giovanni Rovetta's *Salmi concertati* of 1626 lay more emphasis on concertato counterpoint, and an excerpt from *Lauda Jerusalem* shows his facility in weaving a brilliant, modern texture from interesting, contrasted ideas including chromaticism and 'hocket' effects, which are obviously inspired by the unusually vivid textual imagery [Ex. 28]. Rovetta, who in 1627

Ex.28. Rovetta, *Lauda Jerusalem*

Ex.28 (*cont.*)

succeeded Grandi as Monteverdi's assistant at St. Mark's, came strongly under his superior's influence. Monteverdi included a few small-scale psalms in the *Selva morale* of 1641 – the second *Beatus vir* and *Laudate pueri* settings and the third *Confitebor* marked *alla francese*. This last is a most engaging piece with balanced melodies and many paired quavers, scored for a solo soprano with a four-part ripieno that looks forward to the solo concerto concept.[18]

With Lorenzo Agnelli's *Salmi e Messa* of 1637 we have reached the stage of formal organization by the bass, a logical device for unifying long psalm texts, and an improvement on the 'rondo by texture' procedure of Donati's *Confitebor*. Thus the *Laudate Dominum* is built on the descending four-note bass A G F E in triple time, but a much more complex ground plan, one of whose components is none other than the famous *Aria del Gran Duca* theme, is found in *Lauda Jerusalem*. Ostinato schemes pervade the psalms of Tarquinio Merula's *Arpa Davidica* of 1640, which also illustrate his lively, almost instrumentally conceived style. Again, a well-known theme makes an appearance: the litany chant best-known for its use in Monteverdi's *Sonata sopra Sancta Maria* of 1610 provides the alto of *Credidi*, though the fact that any saint may be invoked to the chant shows that this piece was intended to be liturgically adaptable. A similar 'troping' is found in the *Laudate Dominum*, where the alto has the hymn text *Iste confessor*, while the ostinato in the *In convertendo* is harmonic – the note d' sounded throughout by the organ.

Like the motet of similar texture, the four- to six-part psalm was becoming obsolete after 1630. Because of the problems posed by such extended, neutral texts, purely vocal settings in the new style had not lasted long; now the use of obbligato strings became the rule, since choirs were becoming smaller and string players more regularly employed in churches. In a collection of Compline music by Giovanni Battista Chinelli (1639) nearly all the pieces have violin parts, though they are sometimes optional, as in the case of the *sinfonia* to the hymn *Te lucis*. The psalm *Ecce nunc* illustrates the preference for fugal entries (rather than for close imitation), the lively bass line, and the modulations to keys like the mediant minor that point towards the mid-Baroque. It is scored for three voices and two violins, a texture often used for psalm settings which turns up again in some pieces, built on ground basses, in Tarquinio Merula's *Pegaso musicale* (1640).

Certainly, for most composers of psalm settings around 1640 formal organization seemed to be the most pressing need. That even Monteverdi realized this in his last years is evident from his posthumously published *Confitebor* (which exists in two versions for solo and duet with violins respectively),[19] where there is a freely treated ground bass for the verses *and* a violin ritornello; he shows his genius in the variety of melody above the bass and in the occasional, dramatic moments of departure from the expected recurring material. Rovetta, his assistant, used another Monteverdian device (taken from the well-known *Beatus vir* for larger forces) in his psalms – a musical-cum-textual refrain in which both the words and music of the opening are heard at intervals throughout the piece – a technique already tried by Carlo Milanuzzi. For variety's sake, it also became the practice to build a psalm, not on one ground bass, but on several, as in Gasparo Casati's *Laudate pueri* (*Scielta d'ariosi salmi*, 1645). Here, all three currently fashionable ostinati – the 'walking' bass of Monteverdi's *Beatus vir*, the jaunty syncopated chaconne figure of his *Zefiro torna* duet, and the descending four-note bass – are paraded in the order *ABCBCA*, in various keys and with other material interspersed. The style may seem Monteverdian, but it is more likely that it represented the lingua franca of the day, for many composers wrote like this when they introduced ground basses. The use of several such patterns creates a fragmentary rather than a unifying effect typical of Casati, whose music was often unsettled, even nervous in feeling.

Another excellent exponent of this lingua franca was Giovanni Antonio Rigatti, the most gifted of the younger generation at this time, whose *Messa e salmi* of 1640 includes seven psalm settings for one or three voices with violins and continuo, of which the most remarkable is the second *Nisi Dominus*, written over the four-note descending bass. The rich expressiveness of this music derives not just from the incredibly varied melodic activity over the anchoring bass, but also from the many tempo changes specified by Rigatti himself, and integral to his personal style. In the heading to the work he exhorts his performers to apply the utmost flexibility of tempo: 'The opening of this work should be grave, with alterations of tempo in appropriate places as I have advised in the singers' and players' parts, so that the text is matched by as much feeling as possible.' Like Monteverdi in his large posthumous *Laetatus sum* (1650), Rigatti only departs from the ostinato at the 'Gloria Patri', which opens with a submediant major chord (D major) of startling effect, after pages of F major. But there are bold harmonic details all the time, like the rich 7/4 chord of bar 8, which anticipates the vocal entry later (the violin passages are often subtly related the vocal *arioso*) and sounds fresh in a period when the dominant seventh had only just acquired harmonic respectability [Ex. 29a]. Like other

Ex. 29(a). Rigatti, *Nisi Dominus*

inspired practitioners of the ground bass art, Rigatti often dovetails the phrasing of his upper parts with that of the bass, so that at bar 94 there is even one of his characteristic tempo changes in the middle of the bass statement that heralds an anguished, Monteverdian piece of word painting for 'the bread of grief' [Ex. 29b]. The imaginative harmonies of bar 95 can only be interpreted as the sounding of notes dissonant with the bass but in turn held over from bar 94 and anticipating bar 96, another Monteverdian touch. As a whole, there can be no doubt that Rigatti's *Nisi Dominus* belongs to a different stylistic world from the tentative efforts at small concertato psalm settings twenty years earlier; a world where the taut structures of the ground bass and refrain, and the full-scale flowering of *bel canto* triple time were as much a reality in church music as in the operatic *arioso* or the secular madrigal.[20]

Ex.29(b). Rigatti, *Nisi Dominus*

Mass settings: the 'two practices'

From the composer's point of view, the text of the Mass Ordinary stood midway between the motet and the psalm. With the motet it shared the expression of distinct spiritual moods that could be conveyed in music: supplication in the Kyrie and Agnus Dei, praise in the Gloria and Sanctus, and, in the Credo, elements of narrative particularly well suited to expressive treatment, despite the onerous amount of emotionally neutral text dealing with the articles of faith. With the psalm it shared the inherent difficulties of setting long texts (in the Gloria and Credo) required for regular liturgical use. As a result, both *stile antico* and concertato Mass settings flourished side by side in the early years of the seventeenth century. Some composers were not in the least interested in the old idiom, and derived a new approach to the text of the Mass from the early concertato motet. But, for a number of gifted composers, Monteverdi included, the writing of 'da cappella' Masses (as they called them) was a demonstration of their competence in the old contrapuntal manner.[21] For others, of lesser ability, who failed to grasp the modern style and lacked the degree of imagination needed to write in it, the old idiom proved a simple, fail-safe solution to the problem of churches' liturgical needs; they used as a model the *Missa brevis* of the 1580s and '90s, which required little in the way of contrapuntal ingenuity.

Stile antico was generally distinguished from the new style by its *alla breve* notation (though 4/4 did gradually displace this), and a scoring for the chiavette combination (G2 C2 C3 F3) rather than the normal clef combination ubiquitous in concertato works (C1 C3 C4 F4). The various types of Renaissance Mass – cantus firmus, parody, canonic, and 'motto' – persisted into the new century, though (as in psalm settings) the cantus firmus quickly fell out of favour; Adriano Banchieri's *Missa dominicalis* of c. 1600, based on the plainsong Mass *Orbis factor*, is a rare example.[22] The 'motto' Mass, in which a head-motive was the only unifying device, was more common in a period concerned with problems of structure, though in this respect it was more relevant to the concertato Mass. The type that seemed most popular for *stile antico* composers was the parody Mass. The models were sometimes of great antiquity – Monteverdi's Mass on Gombert's *In illo tempore* or Stefano Bernardi's on Arcadelt's *Il bianco e dolce cigno* – but usually were more up to date, and secular; Palestrina's madrigal *Vestiva i colli* was used by Giovanni Battista Biondi and Flaminio Tresti around 1610. An interesting example is Banchieri's *Missa Gloria tua*, based on Monteverdi's madrigal *T'amo mia vita* and therefore in a style transitional between old and new.[23] The reason it bears a Latin title is that the Monteverdi madrigal was issued in Milan in 1607 with the sacred text *Gloria tua* substituted; it is odd that Banchieri, a writer of frolicsome madrigal comedies, should choose to use the 'spiritual' title for his Mass, even though he was a monk.

The only complete Masses by Monteverdi to have come down to us are in the old style and marked 'da cappella' – the parody Mass just mentioned, and the two four-part works written for Venice. In each case, these were published alongside music in the modern style, the Vespers collection of 1610 being the first to juxtapose the 'two practices'. It was not long before others were attempting to display their mastery of both types of Mass composition within a single publication – Pietro Lappi in 1613, Bernardi in 1615,[24] and in the 1620s Donati, Ghizzolo, Gabriello Puliti, Aloisi, and Bellazzi. The difference was between mellifluous, harmonically unadventurous polyphony in the old style, and chordal writing, syllabic quaver movement, ornament, and the interplay of short distinct motifs in the new. Donati is the best of the group – his *Messe* of 1622 were widely sung and went into a third edition within four years. The one modern work in this publication, marked 'in concerto', is a typical 'textural' piece with plenty of contrapuntal interest and little solo melody; *cori spezzati* effects occasionally creep into the tuttis. By contrast, the 'da cappella' Masses show that the old idiom, far from being insipid, was a vehicle for smooth, superbly controlled sonority and counterpoint.[25]

Of the composers who never wrote a note in the *stile antico*, the most important was Grandi, who appended a true concertato Mass to his first motet-book of 1610, scored for ATTB and strongly influenced by Gabrieli. The work is unified by a harmonic progression – F – C – G minor – D – and reaches an expressive climax at the 'Crucifixus', emotionally the high moment of the Mass text [Ex. 30]. Even in such an early work, there is that blend of structural symmetry and spontaneous expression typical of the best Grandi. Other concertato Mass composers who followed him – among them Barnaba Milleville and Salvatore Santa Maria – wrote in a very

Ex. 30. Grandi, *Messa a 4*

ordinary style, with little solo melody and largely syllabic word setting, a means of ensuring comparative brevity in the Gloria and Credo. Lorenzo Agnelli's Mass of 1637 is a good example of how a head-motive, in this case a simple falling scale, could be used to unify a concertato setting. For a more up-to-date style than Agnelli's we need to look to Orazio Tarditi's *Messe in concerto* of 1639. With its bold homophonic opening, the Gloria of one of the five-part Masses in the book has much in common with the breadth of the ceremonial Mass for large forces that was already established by this date. Passages for the solo group have more extended melodies than hitherto, and the texture is more continuous, while tuttis often enter with unexpected harmonies; the majestic slow-moving chords are Monteverdian [Ex. 31].

Ex.31. O. Tarditi, *Messa in concerto*

The Mass in Tarquinio Merula's *Arpa Davidica* of 1640 is, typically for this composer, arranged over a ground bass – not the popular *Aria del Gran Duca* bass mentioned in the heading but in fact the *Ruggiero*. The continuo part has thirty-eight bars of music consisting of five statements of this bass, repeated thirty-five times in all.[26]

By this date, concertato Masses, like psalm settings, tended to be written for a few voices and obbligato violins, as in Chinelli's and Rigatti's publications of 1648. Once again, the purely vocal texture in four to six parts did not have a long lease of life; for those establishments that could afford it, settings using larger forces were more suitable, because they allowed greater variety in the long movements. For many churches, Mass music in *stile antico* was still quite acceptable; Monteverdi's two four-part Masses appeared in 1641 and 1650 respectively, and Francesco Turini issued a collection of *Messe da cappella* in 1643. Such new publications were not, however, the only evidence of this. It is clear that many choirs still possessed choirbooks of sixteenth-century polyphonic Masses; we can presume that they performed these at least as often as Masses composed in later years.

CHAPTER VII

⊙⅋⅋⅋⌒

Large-scale Church Music (I)

The motet: Giovanni Gabrieli and his influence

Giovanni Gabrieli's double-choir style, discussed at the end of Chapter IV, is clearly reflected in the *cori spezzati* music of the generation of composers working in the first decade or so of the new century. That there was less opportunity in provincial cities for the opulence of the Venetian manner is evident from the fact that the scoring does not usually exceed the conventional eight parts, as opposed to Gabrieli's ten- and twelve-part writing. As early as 1601, composers were introducing formal design into motets – ternary shapes in those by Lucio Billi, triple-time refrains in those by Giovanni Battista Stefanini and Francesco Croatti. The refrain might be a tutti with much hemiola rhythm contrasted with 4/4 sections for one choir alone, in a manner similar to the *cantilena* form of the small concertato motet. In Arcangelo Borsaro's *Sit nomen Domini* a tutti refrain is heard five times, interspersed with extended passages for groups drawn from both choirs: Tutti/SSBB/Tutti/SAB/Tutti/ATTB/Tutti/SSABB/Tutti. Borsaro was one of many polychoral composers around the turn of the century whose music became extremely popular in Germany, finding its way into the massive anthologies of Italian motets compiled by (German) collectors like Schadaeus (*Sit nomen Domini* appears in the latter's *Promptuarii musici I* (RISM 1611[1])).

Composers also followed Gabrieli in varying the tessitura of the second choir, and in making the bass lines of each choir agree harmonically, except for a few sonorous moments in rich tuttis. Though quite often homophonic in outline and syllabic in verbal treatment, their motets sometimes resorted to a transitional mixture of imitative and antiphonal writing. Gemignano Capilupi's *Salve radix* (1603) begins very much in the sixteenth-century vein, with imitative entries on a plainsong motif (from the *Salve Regina*) working through all eight voices, before more up-to-date, rapidly overlapping antiphony and delicate cross-rhythms take over; the final, richly detailed plagal cadence is also typical of Gabrieli. The transitional nature of this and other similar music is confirmed by the absence of an organ bass part; where one was provided, it tended merely to be a *basso seguente*. Restrained madrigalisms, such as chromatic inflections or stretches of melismatic writing, would appear when the text invited them, but otherwise the music often seems stereotyped compared with Gabrieli's impressive efforts.

A number of motets by provincial composers stand out above the general mediocrity, even though they are written in a conventional enough way; one such is the *Regina caeli* from Orindio Bartolini's Compline collection of 1613. The Paschaltide Marian antiphon has four short lines of text each ending with an Alleluia, but Bartolini prefers something more subtle than a simple refrain form: for the first Alleluia, a homophonic idea is heard in Choir II in opposition to Choir I's 'laetare'; for the second Alleluia, this idea is passed between the choirs [Ex. 32]. At the third, a completely new triple-time idea is heard with ascending harmonies; and at the fourth, the original idea is recalled before the triple-time motif returns, this time with descending harmonies. Meanwhile, the intervening lines of text display varied approaches to word setting, from pure polyphonic writing to syncopated trumpet motives (at 'resurrexit'), and Bartolini clearly has an excellent feeling for rhythm and sonority.

Ex. 32. Bartolini, *Regina caeli*

Ex. 32 (*cont.*)

Few composers were able to follow Andrea Gabrieli in exploiting the sonorities possible with more than two choirs, and it is no surprise to find that one who did so worked at the music-loving Mantuan court – Benedetto Pallavicino, whose posthumous *Sacrae Dei laudes* of 1605 included two motets for sixteen parts in four choirs. Although his tuttis are never in sixteen real parts (Choirs III and IV doubling the first two), he fully exploits the spatial effects available between groups of differing densities – four, eight, and sixteen parts – to produce exciting music; for him, the four-choir scoring opens up many extra possibilities. The motets could no doubt be realized according to Viadana's instructions, which will be discussed below (pp. 118–19), by mixing the versatile Mantuan instrumentalists with the voices to produce even more delectable results. Pallavicino's position can be contrasted with that of Grandi, who scarcely wrote any double-choir, let alone multi-choral, music at this time, precisely because he was employed at a confraternity whose resources were as modest as the Mantuan court's were lavish. The sole exception to this economy of means, which prevailed in all his published music until he went to Bergamo in 1627, is the eight-part motet *Nativitas tua* in his first motet book of 1610, probably written for a solemn Mass on the feast of the Nativity of the Virgin, an occasion often celebrated in places where there was a devotion to Our Lady. The motet begins with imitations in Choir I, but these are in the concertato, not in the old polyphonic mould; much of the emphasis is on rhythmic panache and purposeful, sequential modulation; Grandi invests his tuttis with a wealth of concertato contrapuntal detail [Ex. 33]. Had he held a post which demanded music like this on a more regular basis, he could well have dominated the field of *cori spezzati* composition as the true successor of Giovanni Gabrieli.

But even for an older, established composer like Giovanni Gabrieli, the *cori spezzati* idiom had already yielded up much of its potential, and in the Venetian's late motets, published in 1615, three years after his death, we can see the transformation from the straightforward polychoral to the mixed concertato style (or, as Bukofzer would have said, 'grand concertato'). Having developed his instrumental idiom in the sonatas and canzonas for the excellent St. Mark's band, he now became one of the first to separate the instruments from the voices and give them obbligato parts in motets, whereas before individual parts could be performed by voices or instruments according to range or groupings at the discretion of the performers. At the same time, he emancipated one or more solo voices from the choir, playing them off against other combinations and writing for them in the more florid manner of the *stile moderno*. His overall aim seems to have been to obtain as great a range of timbre and colour as possible, even if the elements – instrumental participation, the use of solo voices – were not in themselves new.

These elements – the instruments playing their *sinfonie*, the solo voices singing in ornamented fashion (the ornaments could sometimes be regarded

Ex.33. Grandi, *Nativitas tua*

as quite 'instrumental' in idiom)[2] – were fused with the solid writing for full choir or *cappella* to present a great array of mixed vocal and instrumental groups. A motet like *In ecclesiis* – one of Gabrieli's most sumptuous works – illustrates this.[3] It is scored for four soloists, a separate four-part *cappella* or ripieno chorus, six instruments, and continuo. The instruments have a *sinfonia* at one point, and at times accompany the solos and duets as well; the whole piece is bound together by a partly triple-time Alleluia refrain, in which the various sonorities of the preceding episodes are set against the ripieno in a great variety of combinations; and the magnificent effect of the tutti is withheld till near the end. Andrea Gabrieli and his simple polychoral textures have indeed been left far behind. The emphasis on instrumental participation is even more marked in *Jubilate Deo*, for alto, tenor, and eight instruments (two cornetts, five trombones, and bassoon) with optional ripieno, or in *Surrexit Christus* for ATB and eight instruments (two violins, two cornetts, and four trombones), which both have extended, idiomatic passages for the 'band'.

In the double-choir motets of the collection, Gabrieli resorts to other formal designs like *ABB* or *ABAC* as an alternative to refrain schemes. The second setting of *O Jesu mi dulcissime* is cast in the *ABB* form, with a repeated triple-time passage, but it is more interesting as an example of the mood expression – even the beginnings of the baroque theory of 'affections' – that Gabrieli derived from the madrigalian idiom of Marenzio, Gesualdo, and Monteverdi. The use of pungent dissonance and the juxtaposition of very long and very short note-values are just two of the devices that lend musical expressiveness to this motet. There is, certainly, independent writing in the sections for separate choirs, but it is no longer the abstract kind associated with the *prima prattica*; it is conceived vertically, in madrigal fashion, as a sequence of exquisite harmonies. Even the tuttis are not merely chordal – the close canons in the inner voices breathe life and expressiveness into the overall sonority; pure homophony only arrives with the antiphonal triple-time passage at the end. Stylistically, the most important aspect of the motet is the unmistakably concertato part-writing.

In his pioneering study of the composer in 1834, Winterfeld was already fascinated by Gabrieli's use of unorthodox harmonic progressions as a means of expression in these later works.[4] The quest for expression was undoubtedly aided by the confusion in this age of transition from the church modes to the modern idea of tonality – though by comparison with Gesualdo, Gabrieli showed a marked restraint. The sort of harmonic progressions he enjoyed exploiting include tertial harmonic juxtapositions – major chords a major third apart (several examples occur in *O Jesu mi dulcissime*), or a minor third apart (tellingly used in the tutti of *In ecclesiis*). We have seen how such emphasis on chord progression, inherent in the polychoral style, encouraged harmonic awareness, and a feeling for tonality and modulation. Gabrieli's late motets have the strong sense of key common to much concertato music, inasmuch as the strict modality of Renaissance polyphony was left behind; only one tonally ambiguous motet springs to mind – *Hodie completi sunt*, whose F major is coloured by frequent B naturals.

These sumptuous motets of Gabrieli's last years, for all their forward-looking features, stood at the end of an era. After his death in 1612, the large-scale motet generally disappeared from northern Italy. It survived in the work of a few composers who lived in Venice itself, or who found it hard to adapt to the new few-voiced texture. For it was the rapid advance of the small-scale concertato motet, pioneered by Viadana and developed by Grandi and many others, that was responsible for its demise. The provincial composer welcomed the more intimate scorings as being more suitable for the delicate expression of texts which he himself could choose. He might, if he were lucky, still be able to perform double-choir music for psalms and Masses, whose texts were laid down, since the medium provided for some musical variety in long, fixed items. But the provincial musician generally lacked Gabrieli's genius for making large forces compatible with the personal expression of motet texts, so that even on solemn feasts, when he might be certain of having such forces at his disposal, he still preferred the small concertato manner for motets, which at least enabled him to display any talent there might be among his solo singers. Some composers were even less fortunate in that they were only able to mount large-scale music on the greatest feasts. For whereas their choirs had been able to perform music in the grand Venetian manner regularly up to the turn of the century, from 1610 or so many had less to spend on music as a result of inflation or of petty wars between individual states. Music-making at S. Maria Maggiore in Bergamo (to name but one establishment) was transformed by just these pressures. In cities like Bergamo, the arrival of Viadana's practically-conceived type of motet did not come a year too late, and was greeted less as a passport to fashionable expressiveness than as a convenient escape from a tricky financial situation. The large-scale motet managed to survive in wealthier Rome, as the preserve of the practitioners of the so-called 'colossal Baroque'; and also in Germany in the works of Praetorius and Schütz – though, as a result of the hardships of the Thirty Years' War, in the 1630s, even the latter was forced to turn to small-scale textures in his *Kleine geistliche Konzerte*.

Of composers working in Venice, only Giovanni Battista Grillo and Francesco Usper wrote grand motets in the manner of Gabrieli; elsewhere, Capilupi and Bravusi at Modena were among the very few who did so. Giovanni Priuli, though employed at Graz, was very much a Venetian by training, and his *Sacrorum concentuum* (1618–19) contains instrumental canzonas as well as motets. The ten-part *Bonum est confiteri* is related in style to Gabrieli's non-polychoral manner, for the texture is not divided into two choirs, but treated in a freely changing, semi-concertato fashion, with

Ex.34. Priuli, *Bonum est confiteri*

varying voice-groupings that sweep down through the vocal range, and an emphasis on counterpoint rather than melody [Ex. 34]. As in Gabrieli, the tuttis are not fitted into a homophonic strait-jacket. On the whole, this is conservative music; of the composers just mentioned, only Usper and Bravusi introduced independent · instrumental parts in the manner of Gabrieli.

The psalm setting at the beginning of the seventeenth century

The problems of setting long, mostly neutral psalm texts were discussed earlier (p. 98f.). Whereas, in the early years of the new century, few-voiced settings still adopted the conventional idiom of the late Renaissance, those for large forces – where finances permitted the emulation of a splendour Venetian in scale – made use of the developing polychoral style with more than two choirs. Because the large-scale psalm setting did not rely so much on mood painting and expression, the neutrality of the text was less of an obstacle than with smaller textures. The musical and spatial effects of *cori spezzati* lent variety, and the addition of extra choirs gave new dimensions to the medium without prolonging the setting of a long text, since the writing was largely syllabic, with little repetition or time-consuming imitative counterpoint.

Antonio Mortaro and Valerio Bona were among those to publish volumes of Masses and psalms for three and four choirs respectively. Mortaro treated the choirs in the manner of the Gabrielis; phrases of varying length are passed from choir to choir, each one modulating in a new direction or leading to a tutti. Both composers include *falso bordone* settings, which represent the lowest common denominator between polychoral scoring and the simplest rough-and-ready chord sequences. Bona occasionally used a twenty-part texture (four five-part choirs), while Girolamo Giacobbi added a second Magnificat to this 1609 psalm collection laid out for five choirs – SB soloists, two low choirs, one high choir, and one ordinary choir – eighteen parts in all. The emancipation of solo voices was beginning, together with variety of colour and directional effects (the use of two low choirs probably implied contrasted timbres of, say, viols in one and trombones in the other).

One of the most illuminating documents on contemporary performance practice is the preface to Viadana's *Salmi a quattro chori* of 1612, which deserves to be reproduced in full:[5]

The first choir, in five parts, will be situated with the main organ; it will be the principal choir, consisting of five good singers who should sing in the modern manner, confidently and boldly. No instrument, apart from the organ and (if wished) a *chitarrone,* will play with this choir. The organist must take care to use the right stops, according to the markings *v(u)oto* and *pieno.* Whenever members of this choir are singing alone, the organist should play simply and clearly, without diminutions or *passaggi*; but in the ripieno he may play as he pleases, for then he has his opportunity.

The second choir, in four parts, is the *cappella* – the nerve system and very foundation of good music. For this choir, no fewer than sixteen singers are needed. With fewer it will always be a bad *cappella*; with twenty or thirty voices and instruments, it will be a good musical body and will have an excellent effect.

The third choir, in four parts, is a high choir: the first soprano, a very high part, is played by a cornett or violin, the second sung by up to three good soprano voices; the alto, a mezzo-soprano part, is performed by several voices, with violins and curved cornetts; likewise, the tenor is sung by several voices, with trombones, and with violins and organ an octave higher than usual.

The fourth choir, in four parts is a low choir, that is, *a voci pari*: the top part is a very low alto sung by several voices, with violins and curved cornetts an octave higher; the next part is in a comfortable tenor register, sung by a number of voices with trombones; the third part is a baritone – again, this should have good voices or trombones, with violins. The bass is always low, so it should be sung by deep voices with trombones, double-bass viols (*violoni doppi*), and bassoons, with organ an octave lower than normal.

These psalms may be sung by the first two choirs alone. However, if a really fine performance to the people in the modern manner is desired, they may be sung in any number up to eight choirs, by doubling the second, third, and fourth. There is no danger of error in so doing, for the whole affair depends on good singing in the first choir in five parts.

The conductor must stand with this choir, keeping an eye on the organist, watching the movement of the music, and giving entries to the voices. In the ripieni he will turn to face all the choirs, raising his arms as an indication that all are to sing together.

Each choir sings self-contained harmonies, and in the tutti one cannot pick out the octave doubling at all: in my view the music is better this way. Those who wish to avoid these octaves in the ripieni have to use rests, breaks in the music, points of imitation, and syncopations; their music sounds distorted, peasant-like, and garrulous, sung in a headlong rush with little gracefulness.

None the less, I realize that some with senstive ears will object to this novelty, even though others have done the same already. One can see it in print in the *Jubilate* or *Laudate* in sixteen parts by Pallavicino, where soprano and tenor sing twenty-five to thirty bars of consecutive motion. But in conclusion, I have composed in my own way, as others may do, for the present time is one in which he who does the worst seems to do the best. May God be with you.

Viadana's spirited defence of octave doubling, obviously necessary for clarity in polychoral writing, is noteworthy. Treating two of the choirs as more or less dispensable ripieni is a quite new idea which did not become common till around 1630; Viadana's basic texture is double-choir with a concertato Choir I (i.e. consisting only of soloists), to which the reinforcing ripieno choirs are added for purely spatial effects. These can, as he suggests, be made even more splendid by adding extra groups. Musically, these psalms adopt a strictly sectional approach that was becoming popular at the time, and was useful in distinguishing clearly the massive tuttis from the more contrapuntal solo episodes, which were written very much in the style of the *Cento concerti*.[6]

Other composers, far from concentrating the musical argument in the first choir, preferred to draw soloists from both choirs, as in Giacobbi's 1609 psalms, scored for a *coro ordinario* (SATB) and a *coro grave* (alto and three optional trombones, with voices joining in at the tuttis). He tells us that other choirs, of high or low parts according to both resources and the acoustic, may be added, preferably at some distance from the principal ones. Often, the most retrospective writing occurs in the four-part passages; tuttis and solos are more modern, even if the latter are melodically unpretentious. Though there is no overall formal plan, the lively triple-time tuttis begin to resemble refrains, and Giacobbi introduces structural symmetry within some individual verses.

The general freedom of performance in polychoral music extended to the choice of continuo instruments: not only organs but the harpsichord, lute, and *chitarrone* were used to support separated groups. Agostino Agazzari's important treatise *Del sonare sopra il basso* (1607) discusses the realization of the *basso continuo* on such instruments. Adriano Banchieri described the performance of a solemn Mass at Verona one Palm Sunday, in which the continuo group included organ, two *violoni*, two harpsichords, three lutes, and two *chitarroni* – as varied a complement as in Monteverdi's opera orchestra.[7] On occasions like this, special parts would be written out from the 'master' *basso continuo* part-book.

How does the large-scale music in Monteverdi's Vespers of 1610 fit into this picture? Until quite recently, this was the only well-known large-scale sacred music by Monteverdi, let alone by anyone else; part of its fame rested upon the controversy over its liturgical status. Now we have at least become familiar with Monteverdi's more mature, Venetian output, not to mention the later motets of Gabrieli, whose sacred music is wholly available in the collected edition. Kurtzman's work, too, represents a great step forward in the direction of understanding the true stylistic position of the Monteverdi Vespers.[8] A few points of musical interest may be mentioned here.

The opening responses are set most originally, as a conflation of simple *falso bordone* (a conventional device exploited elsewhere in the Vespers)[9] and the toccata-type overture transplanted from *L'Orfeo*, whose brilliant instrumental writing was extremely rare in church music. The *Dixit Dominus* illustrates two formal devices – use of the plainsong psalm tone as a cantus firmus (this occurs in all the psalms and the Magnificat) and the treatment of each verse as a distinct section. The former is unifying and backward-looking, the latter diversifying and forward-looking. To Monteverdi the cantus firmus technique is a challenge, such as chaconne and variation techniques were to become for later composers. In the *Laudate pueri* he weaves melismatic duets around the cantus firmus, or introduces rests to make it fit in with what is happening in the other parts. In the richly-textured *Nisi Dominus*, six parts circumscribe the psalm tone with close canons on scalic and triadic figures – a well-worked Renaissance method of maintaining an overall harmony by 'false' polyphony; though the very slow harmonic movement here sounds old-fashioned, in *Lauda Jerusalem* the psalm tone is broken up into short note-values to fit in with quickly changing harmonies utterly modern in their vitality. The most notable piece in the collection is the larger Magnificat, where sectionalization reappears. Indeed, Monteverdi shuns massed effects, by elaborating the cantus firmus in a succession of little movements which brilliantly exploit various vocal and instrumental groupings in turn: the climax is the extravagant 'Gloria Patri' for echo duet. In Kurtzman's words, this Magnificat contains 'an incredible variety of modern styles and structures, all unified by the severe and unremitting presence of the cantus firmus. The tension between diversity and cohesion, between modernity and conservatism, is even more starkly evident here than in the psalms'.[10] Kurtzman, having systematically examined the psalm and Magnificat repertory in the years before 1610, naturally finds Monteverdi to be far more inventive than a host of minor contemporaries; perhaps more significant is his finding that Monteverdi failed to exert much influence upon those who followed him – a measure of his isolation in a court post at Mantua, where there were resources which the average choirmaster could never hope to enjoy, even on the most solemn occasions.

Though Gabrieli wrote scarcely any Vespers music, to compare the stylistic trends in his large motets with those in the Monteverdi Vespers is to present, perhaps, a more balanced view. We can see at once how conservative a force is Monteverdi's cantus firmus treatment of the psalm tone. The static reciting note pins the harmony down, if not to one chord, then to a circumscribed choice of chords, and usually prevents the deployment of rapidly changing harmonies as developed by the Venetians. Its modal feeling obscures tonal clarity; the repeated reciting note C, for example, can only be harmonized by chords of C, A minor, and F; whereas the possibility of utilizing the dominant (G) is essential for a clear feeling of C major. The long notes and phrases are contrary to the concertato ideal of short, expressive ideas. The wonder is that Monteverdi's music often sounds so fresh, even if one can perceive in it a stylistic struggle. Gabrieli avoided the issue and simply ignored an out-dated technique, so that his late motets sound more assured and in some ways more modern, for all they were written to satisfy a Venetian love of pomp and circumstance.

Both masters were agreed about the importance of the rhythmic element in early baroque style, and both espoused the new ideal of concertato counterpoint with its short, expressive phrases instead of smooth lines and plenty of quasi-canonic interplay. But Gabrieli seems to have had a clearer feel for tonality than Monteverdi, whose hymn *Ave maris stella* is in a very modal D–Dorian without the B♭ key signature (use of the plainsong melody is largely responsible for the modal feeling). For Gabrieli, D minor meant B♭ and C♯, with no ambiguous suggestions of C major and G major. In the psalms, Monteverdi's cantus firmus treatment can beg awkward questions of tonal implication, as in the *Dixit Dominus*; the last two notes of the psalm tone, G and E, are at one point harmonized by the same major chords (G, E) juxtaposed, but the effect is little different from a sixteenth-century false relation in which the *tierce de Picardie* of the final chord contradicts the G♮ of the previous one. It was quite another matter when Gabrieli juxtaposed these two chords in stark, dramatic isolation near the end of *In ecclesiis*, for there he was revelling in the sheer novelty of such a non-functional progression for its own sake. Monteverdi seeks such startling effects by other means – the abrupt change of key from A minor to G minor at the doxology of *Dixit Dominus*, for instance. This is tantamount to an admission of the tonal monotony inherent in cantus firmus composition.

Both Monteverdi and Gabrieli led the way in their use of independent instrumental parts in church music, though Monteverdi demanded more of his players, at least in the responses and large Magnificat. But he was the composer of *L'Orfeo*; Gabrieli had no contact with the operatic manner, and preferred a restrained, solemn sonority from his orchestra.

In the sacred realm, then, Monteverdi is hardly the 'creator of modern music', for his Vespers represents a fascinating transitional stage at which old and new are locked in a struggle which is absent from the smooth stylistic transformation of Gabrieli's music. In many respects it was Gabrieli who most influenced the younger generation. And, in the wider context, what changes had taken place in large-scale church music? A new rhythmic vitality had been born of the predominance of homophony over counterpoint; the modality associated with plainsong was giving way to a feeling of tonality. The idea of two choirs answering one another had flowered into the mixed ensemble with its many combinations of varying texture and pitch, soloists, instruments, and sonorous tuttis. All this conformed to the new ideal of a massive art of colour and space, which enhanced the emotional spirit of Catholicism at the time – in Láng's words, 'a churchly art in which the faithful were uplifted by a mighty architecture and a richly decked clergy, surrounded by pictures and altars of gold and silver and by the music of multiple choirs, orchestras and organs'.[11] This splendid, extravagant music reflected the sensuous, extrovert Jesuit concept of religion.

Further development of the cori spezzati *psalm setting*

Though many choirs suffered a reduction in size after 1610, some were still able to perform double-choir psalms regularly on Sundays, and composers continued to supply them. Their antiphonal, mainly syllabic writing got through long texts efficiently, but began to appear rather conventional in the face of the advancing motet style and the burgeoning mixed concertato. The resulting works fell more and more into the category of *Gebrauchsmusik*: published collections were given Latin titles like *Omnium solemnitatum psalmodia* or simply *Psalmi ad Vesperas* rather than Italian ones to indicate a liturgical compilation as regularly useful as Office and plainsong books.

A few composers, especially those working in and around Milan, a conservative centre somewhat impervious to modern trends, stuck to styles rapidly becoming outdated. Gasparo Villani, for instance, wrote psalms for three choirs in a rich manner that is more Palestrinian than Venetian, with smooth part-writing, plagal cadences, and *stile antico* clef combinations. Giovanni Ghizzolo retained the technique of *falso bordone* in some psalms of 1613, with music resembling Anglican 'double chant', in that the whole antiphonal exchange covers two psalm verses; but *falso bordone*, though it might seem ideal for such functional purposes, was already dying out. Francesco Bellazzi's double-choir psalms of 1618 were conventional – rhythmic homophony for block choirs with a few cross-rhythms and passing notes, but no solo writing. Giacobbi, mentioned earlier (p. 118), had achieved much more variety of scoring in 1609. Leone Leoni came closer to this sort of variety in his psalms of 1613 for choirs of unequal tessitura, which afforded contrasts of vocal colour between SATB and ATTB, but even so, this scoring had been well tried out previously.

The more modern treatment of *cori spezzati* consisted of making the first choir a group of soloists, in which case the psalms would be marked 'con il primo coro concertato' or simply 'concertato'. This idea, expounded by Viadana in his 1612 collection of psalms, differs from that in Gabrieli's motets, which seemed to progress imperceptibly from equal double-, triple-, and quadruple-choir scorings into mixed concertato. Viadana made it quite clear that the first choir consisted of soloists only, in opposition to a great mass of voices and instruments; only in the second choir should there be more than one voice to a part (i.e. ripieno doubling). The element of contrast, between robust solo voices and a mixed *cappella*, would be utterly destroyed by adding voices to the first choir in tuttis.

Just as some early concertato motet composers shunned the art of melody, so one or two who wrote psalms with a concertato first choir (for example Marc'Antonio Negri and Giovanni Battista Tonnolini) refused to give this group anything in the way of solo writing. But Santino Girelli, who included three such psalms in a collection of 1620, did do so, even if the melodies are rather simply written, with the less experienced singer in mind. In these pieces, Girelli tells us in his *avviso*, Choir I must be accompanied by organ (the voices are labelled 'canto organo' and so on in the part-books), whereas Choir II need not be; this would seem to support the contention that the former consisted of soloists throughout, requiring continuous organ accompaniment, while the latter might be separated and doubled by instruments (a second organ part is, however, notated in the continuo part-book).[12] In the *Dixit Dominus*, the solo textures of Choir I alternate with tuttis which have varied antiphonal writing, frequent chordal canons, massive imitative entries, and sometimes dramatic opposition between one voice and the tutti [Ex. 35]. (Note also how Girelli draws soloists from the second choir in order to play off different equal-voice duet combinations.) At the doxology, he refers to a plainsong psalm tone as a token gesture of reverence for the past – gone are the days of whole psalms built on a plainsong cantus firmus. His concept of two separated choirs, with soloists drawn from both, points towards the mixed concertato; it is distinct from the ripieno concept, from which antiphonal writing came to be altogether purged. A fusion of the two occurs in Lappi's Compline music of 1626 for three and four choirs: in the sixteen-part Nunc dimittis, tuttis alternate with a series of equal-voice duets which require a voice each from the first two choirs (Choir III is a low-pitch choir).

Grandi only ventured into the field of large-scale psalm writing at the end of his life, partly as a result of his position at Bergamo. His collection *Salmi a8 brevi con il primo coro concertato* (1629) is clearly intended for regular use at Vespers, economy of means being implied by the word 'brevi'. Thus, the *Laudate Dominum*, even allowing for its extremely short text, runs to only 38

Ex. 35. Girelli, *Dixit Dominus*

bars. The composer's problem is quite the reverse of the usual one of coping with a long, shapeless text; Grandi provides ample variety within a short space, contrasting in turn triple-time antiphony (solo versus ripieno), recitative-like solos, and a fugal interlude for solo choir. This is planned so that the doxology enters with an abrupt return to joyous homophony (its arrival was often signalled by sudden tuttis, key-changes, and the like) [Ex. 36]. This passage, with its circle-of-fifths modulations and unexpected B^b chord at 'et Spiritui', is no longer novel, but recalls the manner of the long-dead Gabrieli. Greater originality is found in Grandi's second *Dixit Dominus* from this collection; but as this setting is really a mixed concertato work, it will be discussed further on.[13]

By the 1620s, straightforward antiphonal writing was becoming obsolete

Ex. 36. Grandi, *Laudate Dominum*

in large-scale psalms, the function of the second choir being eroded until it merely supplied reinforcement in tuttis. Thus, both Giovanni Ghizzolo's 1619 psalms and Aurelio Signoretti's 1629 psalms are marked 'a5 or a9'; the first choir, of five parts, is a concertato group with varied textures, whereas the remaining four parts are a purely optional ripieno, added at sporadic climactic points in the music with different chord-spacing for sonorous effect.[14] The dispensable ripieno had supported the *cappella* in Viadana's polychoral psalms; now it supported the soloists. Grandi's posthumous large-scale publication of 1630 (*Raccolta terza*, assembled by Simonetti, a friend and singer at St. Mark's) consists mainly of psalms in which a few soloists – mostly low voices – are joined at tuttis by a ripieno and sometimes by instruments (cornetts or trombones) to produce a kind of 'rondo by texture' related to the concertato motet. This scheme was most appropriate in sectional works, where short movements could be varied in tempo and style as well as in texture, along the lines of the *cantilena* motet. In these psalm settings the tuttis form a proper refrain binding the whole structure together. An example occurs in Grandi's *Nisi Dominus* for SAT_1T_2 soloists, trombones (which play in both tuttis and solos), and SATB ripieno, whose groundplan is

Nisi Dominus	S & T_1 duet
Nisi . . . custodierit	A & T_2 duet
Vanum est vobis	Tutti
Cum dederit	T & 3 trombones
Sicut sagittae	Tutti
Beatus vir	SAT_1T_2 soloists
Gloria Patri	AT & 3 trombones
Sicut erat	Tutti

The tutti frequently contains the chord progression G–C–A–D.[15] We can compare this with the first *Confitebor* of Monteverdi's *Selva morale*, the only psalm in that collection to use the simple ripieno scheme.[16] The ATB soloists always sing together in the lilting triple time which was rapidly becoming favoured for long texts and even for whole pieces by this time, with quaver rather than crotchet movement (in 3/4 values); the tuttis, in solemn 4/4, add five ripieno voices and, as in Grandi, are based on a recurring harmonic progression – G–A–F–G–Eb–F, with G minor cadence – to produce a satisfying rondo form.

Even after 1630, however, a few composers were giving isolated passages to the second choir alone, usually to exploit a contrast of colour if its tessitura was different from that of the first choir; in such music Choir II was not altogether dispensable. In Giovanni Rovetta's 1644 psalms, the pure homophonic antiphony was still more anachronistic – in reality *stile antico* writ large, and appropriate for days when double-choir psalms were required at St. Mark's, where Rovetta had recently become *maestro*. Just as scorings with obbligato instruments were ousting purely vocal ones in small-scale psalm settings, so the plain *cori spezzati* style was increasingly yielding ground to the mixed concertato in large-scale psalm settings. It might even be argued that the real heyday of polychoral style was not the early seventeenth but the late sixteenth century. There was not a great deal to add to what the Gabrielis had achieved by 1600, so it was to be expected that progressive composers would transform the function of separated choirs into something resembling the strict scheme of the later concerto grosso.

An alternative course, followed mainly by composers outside northern Italy, was to magnify the polychoral idea into the 'colossal Baroque', a style in which much of the music's essence consists of spatial and colouristic effects for their own sake; sometimes there was not much distinction between instrumental and vocal writing, or much melodiousness in solo passages. Some of the massive German motets in Praetorius's *Polyhymnia* of 1619 show this tendency; the vocal ornamentation is of the complex, non-melodic sixteenth-century type, even if the instrumental parts for violins and cornetts are admittedly more brilliant than in most Italian music. Contrast this music with Schütz's *Psalmen Davids* of the same year, whose layout in four-choir pieces is just that of Viadana's 1612 psalms, and whose style is obviously related to that of Venice.[17] The 'colossal Baroque' caught on in Rome. Elsewhere, its use was most effective on very grand occasions, such as the consecration of Salzburg Cathedral in 1628, when a *Te Deum* for twelve choirs by Stefano Bernardi was performed.[18] It was still very much alive in the same city, in an updated form using a greater variety of instrumental groupings, in what we have come to know as the *Missa Salisburgensis* (?1682), formerly attributed to the Roman Orazio Benevoli.

❦

CHAPTER VIII

Large-scale Church Music (II)

The emergence of the mixed concertato in psalms

The term 'mixed concertato' generally implies music in which the textures and groupings change freely throughout, as opposed to music for distinct, separated choirs. Obbligato parts for instruments are usually an essential feature of the score in mixed concertato; if they are not, instruments would still participate by either doubling or replacing some vocal lines, as is suggested in those late Gabrieli motets where all parts have words underlaid but only some are marked 'voce'. Since the performance of a large 'orchestral' psalm was a considerable undertaking impossible in most cities except on big feasts, the mixed concertato scoring was slow to become established in psalms.

Once again, the large Magnificat of Monteverdi's Vespers seems to have provided a most original demonstration of what could be achieved, even if few composers were in a position to do likewise. One who did was Giovanni Francesco Capello, whose Holy Week compilation of 1612 includes a setting of the psalm *Miserere mei Deus* for voices and a most colourful string ensemble of four bowed instruments and two *chitarroni*, which provide ritornellos and sonorous accompaniments to vocal sections in a thoroughly modern manner.[1] The next important publication was Amadio Freddi's *Messa, vespro e compietà* of 1616, which also represented a fresh approach to psalm composition, free from Monteverdi's cantus firmus practice; with its obbligato violin and cornett parts above the five voices, it was more colourful and varied in treating neutral texts than, say, a five-part voices-only scoring. The opening of *Nisi Dominus*, for instance, presents four successive colour groupings – AT duet, tenor and instruments, five-part voices, and an imitative tutti for 'surgite', which shows craftsmanlike imitation and inversion of the text-inspired rising scale phrase [Ex. 37]. That Freddi is a good melodist can be seen from the widely modulating soprano line at 'cum dederit' (bar 46). Formally, the whole psalm is unified by a number of recurring ideas, among them a harmonic progression marked 'x' below the continuo in Ex. 37, and the rising scale phrase mentioned above, which makes a very prominent return at the lively 'Sicut erat'. Here the idiomatic instrumental parts over repeated choral chords strongly recall the opening of Monteverdi's Vespers of 1610.[2] In all

Ex.37. Freddi, *Nisi Dominus*

Ex. 37 (*cont.*)

the works of Freddi's 1616 volume, the scoring for two high instruments above a five-part choir anticipates what was to become the norm much later in all but the most grandiose large-scale music, which still required the sonority of trombones. Freddi's fairly light textures have less in common with the solemn grandeur of late Gabrieli than with the few-voiced motet.

By contrast, the Venetian quest for a dignified style with the widest possible variety of sonority in grand concertato music is reflected in Ignazio Donati's *Salmi boscarecci* (1623), a most interesting and ambitious psalm collection. This was Donati's one proper large-scale compilation; when it appeared, he was a choirmaster at his native town of Casalmaggiore in Lombardy. It is written out in twelve part-books and a *basso continuo*; the first six books contain parts for SSATTB soloists, while into the other six are compressed parts for a further six solo voices, ripieni, and instruments (three violins and three trombones). The preface, which is as illuminating for mixed concertato performance as Viadana's 1612 preface was for polychoral, outlines so many possibilities that this must be dubbed 'do-it-yourself' music *par excellence*. Donati explains:[3]

I have been persuaded by my superiors, kind readers, to publish this work; I have called it 'Sylvan psalms' since it will, in my view, serve for lesser feasts. I have thought it necessary to make some suggestions, for it is a work large in format and capable of being performed in different ways, with few, or many parts. To save myself tiring work, and to limit its cost, I have however compressed it into twelve books (apart from the organ bass).

First, then, one may use the first six books to sing the music with six solo voices. Parts may be transposed: if sopranos are scarce, the first soprano may be sung by tenors. If nuns wish to sing it, they may transpose the bass part up an octave to make an alto part.

Second, the other six books, called 'ripieno', contain six more voices which also sing *in concerto*, and six instruments, three low and three high. One may use some or all of these vocal and instrumental parts at will, to make up another choir in the choirstalls; one may double the voices only in the passages marked tutti.

Third, if one wishes to make up more choirs, one may place SSAB of the first choir with the organ, the first tenor with the low instruments as a second choir, and the second tenor with the high instruments as a third choir. If there are several copies of these books, one may also add two further choirs, one made up of three voices and other low instruments, the other of three high instruments and their voices. Voices may be doubled in tutti passages. If necessary, the last-mentioned soprano parts may both be sung by tenors. One could, alternatively, make a fourth choir out of the second six books to sing in tuttis. All this is at the taste and judgement of whoever is pleased to avail himself of this work.

Fourth, if one wishes to use the last six books for both voices and instruments, it should be noted that where it says solo, only the singer should sing, and where it says trombone or violin, only the instrument should play; in passages marked tutti, they both sing and play in unison. But if either a solo voice or instrument uses one of them, they should take care to sing or play at the right moment. . .

Such is the freedom of the performer that a score discloses but half the actual sound of the music, the overall impression of which would be considerably affected by the spatial disposition of the performers. What can be said is that, far from relying on the mode of performance to lend individuality to the music through mere gimmickry, Donati has deliberately written the music in such a way that the spatial effects will enhance it in circumstances where they can be arranged, while at the same time maintaining enough intrinsic musical interest for an entirely plain performance to succeed. This is no mean feat; it is achieved by such devices as ornamented references to plainsong psalm tones, striking harmonic juxtapositions, inventive word painting, dramatic silences, little sub-sections with symmetrically disposed textures or cadence keys, and the considerable contrapuntal complexity of some tuttis, where the six soloists maintain their independence in the face of solid homophony. There is no overall structural conception, rather an inexorable alternation of tuttis and kaleidoscopically varied solo groupings – the 'rondo by texture' writ large – sometimes moving through various related keys to prevent tonal monotony. Some of these features are well illustrated in an extract from the Magnificat included in the collection, particularly the ornamental duet writing of 'fecit potentiam' (as ornate as Donati gets in such practically-conceived music) [Ex. 38]. These psalm settings owe less to Monteverdi than to Gabrieli, whose *In ecclesiis* paved the way for such explorations of sonority without demanding the virtuosic instrumental playing of Monteverdi's Mantuan musicians. But here the score is little more than a blueprint for performance; if we followed Donati's instructions for performing it with five separated choirs, the sound would be remarkably scattered, for the suggested groupings do not fit rigidly the textures of the music. Donati's concern is not with vocal or instrumental brilliance but with sheer sonority, balance of key, and stereophonic effect where possible. For those unable to muster twelve soloists, six-part ripieno, and instruments, he hastens to make it clear that the resources could be watered down without spoiling the musical substance.

Ex. 38. Donati, Magnificat

Only one or two of the psalms that Grandi published after he had gone to Bergamo belong to the mixed concertato category. One is the *Dixit Dominus* from the 1629 volume of double-choir psalms discussed earlier, in which parts for violin and viol (or trombone) are added to the solo and ripieno choirs. Clearly the most notable feature of this psalm is its sectional plan; like Monteverdi's 1610 Magnificat or Viadana's 1612 psalms, it consists of short movements, scored for various combinations, each working out distinctive musical ideas – in contrast to Donati's method of continuous textural variation. In this respect it heralds the baroque cantata. The two instruments fulfil varied functions: in tuttis they side with one or other choir (perhaps suggesting a position separated from both), the violin adding an extra *acuto* line and the viol doubling the continuo, while in solo movements they enter into graceful dialogue with the melodious vocal line [Ex. 39]. This is, of course, the style of the *motetti con sinfonie*, in which

Ex. 39. Grandi, *Dixit Dominus*

Grandi had by now gained much experience. The most original use of the instruments occurs in the warlike verse 'dominus a dextris', especially at the words 'conquassabit capita', where Grandi adopts the dramatic *stile concitato* with its static harmonies and string tremolos no doubt inspired by Monteverdi's *Combattimento*, which he may well have admired while at Venice.[4] Leandro Gallerano's *Messa e salmi* of 1629 is like Grandi's late publications in that it contains a mixture of *cori spezzati* music with a dispensable ripieno, and mixed concertato items with essential instrumental parts. Thus in some pieces the ripieno choir and the instruments are optional, so that the music may be performed simply in five parts, or more lavishly in nine, with instruments added.

How do these psalm settings compare with those in Monteverdi's *Selva morale*, published in 1641, but containing the fruits of several decades of composition? The absence of a clear chronology for his psalm settings is regrettable, but the developments which have been outlined above may help to place them more clearly in perspective. In terms of structure, Monteverdi was one of the first composers to organize psalm settings by the introduction of repeated musical material. Whether the settings were sectionalized or not was irrelevant, since, although the practice of having separate movements for each verse might seem to anticipate the cantata, it equally had roots in the old *alternatim* psalm of the previous century; indeed, of Monteverdi's mixed concertato pieces, only the Magnificat is sectional – the seven psalms are all through-composed. The two settings of *Dixit Dominus* have no formal organization at all, consisting as they do of a succession of musical tableaux which might include pictorial elements when the text gave opportunity (e.g. the trumpet motifs at 'inimicos tuos' in the first setting).[5] This free sequence of varied scorings is similar, though on a broader scale, to the progressive form of the small-scale concertato motet, which was always through-composed. The third *Laudate Dominum* is also in a free form, apart from the recapitulation of the dance-like opening duet by the tutti half way through.

The refrain element appears in the first *Laudate Dominum*, in which a low, modulating tutti occurs near the beginning, and again at the 'Sicut erat'. A more balanced ternary shape, with central section in triple time, is found in the well-known first *Beatus vir*, but in addition there are rondo elements in the recurrence throughout the psalm, of the opening bars (with their text) and of violin phrases which are derived from the madrigal *Chiome d'oro*, published in 1619. The first *Laudate pueri* and the second *Laudate Dominum* have a basic rondo form with themes and ideas recurring consistently throughout. All these works were very probably written after 1625; this was the time when Grandi developed the rondo form of his motets with instruments, while acting as Monteverdi's assistant at Venice. Carlo Milanuzzi, also working there, followed the trend and, as we saw in Chapter VI, introduced rondo structures into his two- and three-part psalm settings of 1627. The use of a leisurely triple time with plenty of rhythmic variety also points to a date later than 1625 for these Monteverdi works.

As regards instrumental writing, the resemblance between the violin styles of Monteverdi and Grandi (in his motets with violins) suggests that, in general, these mixed concertato psalms were composed after 1620 or so, when the genre was in its early stages. Whereas in the 1610 Vespers Monteverdi's violin style had been derived from *L'Orfeo*, here it is altogether more restrained, and contributes to the melodic development. Moreover, the changing make-up of the St. Mark's orchestra was reflected in the fact that he no longer used the cornett for obbligato parts, though he did specify optional trombones in certain works.[6]

Monteverdi's vocal ornamentation, though still often elaborate, had changed too. In the Vespers it had been virtuosic and extravagant; now it enhanced the melodic outline. We can see this by comparing the 'Gloria Patri' verses of the large-scale Magnificats of 1610 and 1641. In the earlier work, the tenor parts have mere decoration, pure passage-work, with no particular regard for what is going on elsewhere; in the later setting, the ornaments fit naturally into a sequential triple-time melody. Other examples of elaborate 'Gloria Patri' verses in the *Selva morale* psalms (the first *Laudate pueri*, the third *Confitebor*) are disciplined either by four-bar phrasing or by logical harmonic progressions.

As has been mentioned in Chapter V, publishing in Venice was badly hit by the plague of 1630, and was almost brought to a halt for five years so that the next important collections of large psalm settings did not appear until the end of this troubled decade. The two most interesting compilations were both by Venetian composers, Giovanni Rovetta and Giovanni Antonio Rigatti, who both, like Monteverdi, experimented with rondo, ternary and now ground bass forms. For instance, the many repeating elements in Rovetta's *Confitebor* (*Messa, e salmi*, 1639) build up into a complex rondo form:

A	Ritornello I	violins	E'	Memor erit	B_1, violins
B	Confitebor	T; SSB	F	Ut det illis	SSTB, violins
A	Ritornello I	violins	C	Fidelia	tutti
B	Magna opera	T; ATB	E	Ritornello II	violins
A	Ritornello I	violins	E''	Redemptionem	B_2; tutti
C	Confessio	tutti	G	Intellectus	TB
D	Misericors	all voices	F	Gloria	SSTB, violins
E	Ritornello II	violins	C	Sicut erat	tutti

The first part of the psalm (*ABCD* in the table) is mainly in triple time, after which the metre alternates between triple and duple. Besides violin ritornellos, Rovetta sometimes used musical-cum-textual refrains in which both the words and music of the opening are heard, as did Monteverdi, whose 'troping' could make nonsense of the Latin text despite utter logic in the music. Rovetta also built sections on ground basses – sometimes several different ones, and sometimes as long as eleven bars. Monteverdi was doing the same, though in his case this was a by-product of opera and the concertato madrigal; the most memorable example of ostinato in his church music occurs, with a four-note figure G–G'–c–d, in the superb *Laetatus sum* published posthumously in 1650 and probably a late work.[7]

The small-scale *Nisi Dominus* from Rigatti's *Messa e salmi* of 1640 was discussed earlier (pp. 104–5); what is remarkable about this publication as a whole is its similarity in breadth and comprehensiveness to Monteverdi's *Selva morale* of the following year, with its large-scale concertato Mass and psalms, smaller works for a few solo voices and instruments, and *da cappella* settings. The Magnificat of Rigatti's collection, scored for seven-part choir and five-part orchestra, is a work as massive in scale as Monteverdi's largest psalms. Traces of the latter's influence include the slow chords at 'quia respexit', or at 'et misericordia'. The pungent tertial relationships between F and D major, G and E major, set a word that Monteverdi himself would never let pass without some illustrative device. But the most interesting part of the work is what Rigatti calls a 'toccata da guerra' at the verse 'Fecit potentiam', where a dramatic tenor recitative alternates with exciting instrumental 'battle music', actually marked 'istromenti in battaglia'. This recalls Monteverdi's *Combattimento* and his *madrigali guerrieri* published just two years earlier, in 1638, though never yet, so far as is known, introduced into church music with such abandon [Ex. 40]. It is surely no coincidence that this passage occurs at one of the few points in the Magnificat text that invites pictorial effects. For the qualities in which Rigatti most excels – melodic grace and variety, and subtle structural imagination – an even finer work is the second *Confitebor*, for six-part choir, two violins, and four optional viols.[8] This is bound together by the alternation of two ritornellos, one vocal and one for violins, and by the return of the opening music at 'Sicut erat'. An astute stroke is the triple-time variation of the violin ritornello at its fourth appearance, beautifully forestalling the listener's expectations and leading to a suave, romantic passage with expressive tempo changes. Elsewhere, the melodies are rhythmically taut and sometimes quite angular, but always delightfully original.

Other contributors to the large psalm repertory include Tarquinio Merula, Maurizio Cazzati, and Nicolò Fontei. Merula's collection of 1639 and Fontei's of 1647 both contain a mixture of large-scale psalms, small-scale ones, and some marked 'pieno' (equivalent to *da cappella*); the resources of the big pieces vary from between five and eight voices and between two and five instruments, the violins among the latter usually being the only obbligati. Cazzati's 1641 collection, one of the first in his distinguished career as a mid-century church musician, was scored for just five-part choir with two violins – a workaday combination that was becoming increasingly well established. The concertato psalm without instruments was dying out; the new grouping combined the possibilities of

Ex.40. Rigatti, Magnificat

the old type with the brilliance of violins (and by now most city churches had two resident violinists). Up-to-date stylistic features of this music included a greater variety of rhythmic movement in both triple and 4/4 time. The former had developed from the unrelenting *tactus inaequalis* of earlier years to something more flowing, with dotted minims and quavers (in 3/4 time), while the latter presents semiquavers in figuration rather than as ornaments. Cazzati also emphasized key relationships in a new way by the use of pedal points.

The large-scale Mass

Large-scale Masses can be discussed under one heading since on the whole, fewer of them were written than were psalms, which were always required in batches to fulfil the needs of the Office. The writing of large Masses was often avoided altogether by those who stuck to the *stile antico* for settings of the Ordinary; others usually appended one or two to their large psalm compilations – hence the frequently encountered title *Messa e salmi*.

The broad, solemn style of such Masses has its roots in those Mass movements by Giovanni Gabrieli published posthumously in 1615, in which instrumental participation is taken for granted if not actually specified. An excellent example is the Sanctus for three choirs of varying tessitura, built on simple musical ideas like rising sixths, 'Phrygian' cadences, and choral antiphony; at the triple-time 'Hosanna' the bass has pairs of falling fourths – a device much used later by Monteverdi – which modulate continuously beneath a superb 'textural crescendo'.[9] Works like this, and indeed large-scale Masses in general, were probably intended for especially solemn feasts. This three-choir scoring appears in Antonio Mortaro's Masses published in 1608; the resulting music is grander than most Mass music of the previous century and more impressive than the antiphonal double-choir Masses that appear in the roughly contemporary motet collections of Lucio Billi, Andrea Bianchi, and Francesco Croatti.

Perhaps the earliest genuinely 'orchestral' Mass is that in Giovanni Francesco Capello's *Motetti et dialoghi* of 1615, which is also quite exceptional for its incorporation of material from pre-existing *instrumental* music (two canzonas by Mortaro); it is scored for three voices and five instruments. A more conventional balance is found in Amadio Freddi's 1616 Mass for five-part choir, with violin and cornett, which play solo and duet *sinfonie* at the opening of the Kyrie. This illustrates how the customary extra-liturgical instrumental music at Mass became part of the Ordinary setting itself. Ercole Porta's Mass of 1620 adds to the five-part choir a full five-part orchestra of two violins and three trombones. This is an unusually impressive work to have emanated from the small provincial town of Persiceto, where Porta directed the music (he may have studied with the progressive Girolamo Giacobbi in nearby Bologna). Nevertheless, the instrumental writing is simple, and involves a certain amount of doubling in the voices, though it is noticeable that, in places, the instruments play unadorned versions of the more ornate vocal parts which are especially effective on trombones.[10]

Porta's fine feel for textural contrasts is illustrated in the build-up from the 'laudamus te' duet to the 'gratias' tutti [Ex. 41], while he is not averse to distant modulations, or to such striking progressions as that at 'vivos et mortuos' (C minor–A major). Like Freddi, Porta incorporates instrumental sections into the Mass setting, notably a *sinfonia* of twenty-eight bars tellingly placed after the declamatory 'Crucifixus' and brilliant 'Et resurrexit' sections of the Credo; this recalls the placing of the *sinfonia* in the centre of Gabrieli's *In ecclesiis*.

The limited number of examples indicates that the mixed concertato Mass had barely caught on in the provinces by 1620, and some composers still wrote for eight-part choir without obbligato instruments. Giovanni Priuli's *Missa Sancti Benedicti* is hardly even antiphonal, though it does make play with a series of equal-voice duets,[11] but one of his 1624 Masses includes parts for violin, cornett, and trombone, whose writing is most ornate and

Ex.41. Porta, *Messa concertata*

decorative. Giulio Bruschi's 1627 Mass, like Grandi's 1629 psalms, is written in *cori spezzati* style, with Choir I consisting of soloists, and is held together by a motto idea. Its Credo ends in triple time, yet another mark of the increasing emancipation of that metre found in the most progressive music of this date (e.g. Grandi's late motets of 1630).

By this time the 'dispensable' ripieno had appeared in the large-scale Mass, just as in psalm settings. Gallerano's 1629 Mass requires two violins and *chitarrone* in the Kyrie and Gloria, but not in the rest of the work; the ripieno is optional throughout. In Milanuzzi's *Missa primi toni* (1629), both ripieno and instruments are optional, and only appear in the Gloria, Credo, and Agnus II, where they reinforce the three soloists with relatively independent parts involving unobtrusive crossrhythms. The Mass is nevertheless marked 'for three voices', indicating that only the soloists are essential; such a piece could be used where there was a mere handful of singers, as well as for festive occasions when larger resources were available.

The large-scale Mass of 1630 is Grandi's most ambitious work.[12] Only months after his death from the plague it was published in a collection gathered together by his Venetian friend Simonetti, the psalms of which were mentioned earlier (p. 127); Simonetti evidently had difficulty in understanding its precise scoring, and scattered the parts among the twelve part-books of the publication without rhyme or reason. Clearly, it was written for some solemn occasion at S. Maria Maggiore in Bergamo – probably Assumption Day, the church's principal festivity. Documentary evidence, in the form of the roll of regular musicians and lists of payments to others hired from outside, shows that the right kind of forces were assembled on this feast (15 August) in both 1627 and 1628. In 1627 there were present twenty-eight singers, two cornetts, one violin (doubling trombone), two trombones, two bassoons, two *violoni*, four organs, and two conductors; in 1628 there were no fewer than fifty-seven musicians in all, including two virtuoso singers from the Mantuan court (Francesco Dognazzi and Andrea Pisani) who sang two of the solo parts. Even so, the Mass was published in as adaptable a form as possible, to suit varying resources and needs. It lacks a Sanctus and Agnus Dei for the liturgical reasons considered in Chapter III.

The Kyrie is a straightforward four-part movement in F, in a style quite distinct from Grandi's late psalms. Over a chaconne-like bass come entries of an ornamental descending theme reminiscent of Monteverdi, which is freely inverted at the 'Christe' [Ex. 42a, b]. Between Kyrie and Gloria

Ex.42(a & b). Grandi, *Messa concertata*

Grandi interpolates two extra-liturgical pieces characteristic of the large-scale ceremonial Mass. Though it may well have been the custom to preface the priest's intonation of the Gloria with a short organ piece (*intonazione*, indeed) announcing the key to be used, it was something quite new to have both a specially-composed instrumental sonata and an antiphonal *sinfonia* setting the words of the intonation. The sonata seems to lack a middle part and an organ bass; it was probably written for three trombones, a most unusual but effective sonority. The *sinfonia* helps us determine the spatial disposition of forces for the Gloria, suggesting that the two sopranos should be separated from the cornett and trombone to produce the maximum contrast of direction, colour, and rhythms.

The Gloria and Credo are on a large scale, for roughly similar forces: two distinct solo groups and a ripieno group. In the Gloria, the solo groups consist of two sopranos versus alto, tenor, and two trombones; in the Credo, SSB versus alto and three trombones.[13] In both, the ripieno choir, called *cappella* in the part-books, consists of ATTB, but in the Gloria this is augmented by violin and cornett parts, making it effectively a six-part group. The style of these two movements is extremely simple – short, monolithic chordal tuttis punctuating imitative passages for the solo groups. Yet there is a continual and logical flow of musical ideas across the textural contrasts. The simple 'Phrygian cadence' progression at the beginning of Ex. 43 provides an anchoring idea for a large middle section of the movement starting at 'Domine Fili', around which revolve various ideas (e.g. the passionate 'miserere' in bar 66) [Ex. 43]. At the end of the example, bars 62–71 are recapitulated at 'Qui sedes'. The formal organization of this

Ex.43. Grandi, *Messa concertata*

Ex.43 (*cont.*)

middle section is remarkably similar to that in Monteverdi's Gloria from the *Selva morale*, an isolated large-scale Mass movement scored for seven-part choir and two violins:[14]

	Grandi	Monteverdi
Domine Deus	Group I then II	Soprano duet
Pater omnipotens	Group II	Tutti
Domine Fili	Tutti	Soprano duet
Jesu Christe	Group I	Tutti
Domine Deus	Group I then II	Soprano duet
Agnus Dei	Group II	Tutti
		Violin ritornello
Qui tollis	Tutti (to C major)	Group I
miserere	Soprano solo	Violin ritornello
Qui tollis	Tutti (to G major)	Group II
suscipe	Group I then II (3/4)	Violin ritornello
Qui sedes	Tutti major)	Group III
miserere	Soprano solo	

Though a rising motive in the bass makes several appearances, there is no similar degree of formal organization in Grandi's Credo; instead, interest resides in the most expressive kernel of the movement [Ex. 44]. The 'Crucifixus', for solo tenor, is remarkable for being the first self-contained monody in a Mass setting and, though only twenty-three bars long, is as fine a piece of writing as any by this composer of solo motets *par excellence*. Particularly exquisite are the repetition of the first phrase, shortened and at a lower pitch; the impassioned syncopations of 'passus'; and the final ornamentation and II–I cadence.

There were few publications containing large Masses in the lean post-plague years. Orindio Bartolini, rather surprisingly, brought out two in 1633 and 1634, which suggests that his choir at Udine Cathedral was still of reasonable size. The inclusion of a Requiem and *Te Deum* in the first of these may well have been connected with the commemoration of the plague's victims and the thanksgiving for its end. The style of the Masses

Ex.44. Grandi, *Messa concertata*

Ex.44 (cont.)

is a little conservative, with solos drawn from both of the separated choirs, which are almost equal in importance. The 'ripieno' Mass, with optional second choir, appears in Giacomo Ganassi's 1634 collection, in which the tuttis often have continuous counterpoint for the soloists against homophony in Choir II, whose presence would considerably alter the music's effect.

The Mass of Giovanni Rovetta's 1639 *Messa, e salmi* (dedicated to Louis XIII of France) shows a strong Monteverdian influence, and reflects the changing musical language of the 1630s – for instance, the sound of the 6/3 chords at the opening of the Kyrie, the modulation from G minor to its relative major, and the smooth, conjunct motion of the bass line [Ex. 45]. The Kyrie is scored for the frequently-chosen five-part choir with violins, typical of this period; Rovetta adds a sixth voice in the Gloria and a seventh in the Credo, and there is no Sanctus or Agnus Dei. The two large movements are well varied in their musical ideas and textures, with a certain amount of formal organization in individual sections. There is a definite similarity in the movements' groundplans, for in each, the first half is dominated by a rondo of repeated ideas (bass lines in the Gloria, tuttis and melodic shapes as well in the Credo); each has a central section for low solo voices, a rather dry *stile antico* section in five parts, and an extended triple-time passage. The Monteverdian influence can be seen in the falling-fourths bass (C–G–A–E–F–C), heard several times in the Gloria,[15] and even more at the opening of the Credo (cf. the 'Domine Deus' tutti of the Monteverdi Gloria), though Rovetta cleverly varies this passage with

discordant clashes when he recalls it at 'et expecto' [Ex. 46]. Though the large-scale Mass repertory was fairly restricted in the early seventeenth century, it seemed from the beginning to boast a greater stylistic assurance than was characteristic of the groping development of the psalm. Venice's

Ex.46(a & b). Rovetta, *Messa concertata*

Ex.46(b)

supremacy in the field of the 'ceremonial' Mass lasted for half a century and beyond, throughout the incumbencies of Monteverdi, Rovetta, and Cavalli, as *maestri* at St. Mark's and the Venetian ideal inspired the Masses of Capello, Grandi, and others early in the century, as it did those of Rigatti (1640), Cazzati (1641, 1653, 1660), and Orazio Tarditi (1648) later on. The Venetian tradition was maintained by Cavalli's well-known *Messa concertata* of 1656.[16] The 'orchestral' Mass, as it could now be called, was indeed the one type of big mixed concertato music to survive through the middle and late baroque period by shifting both north to Austria and south Germany (whose Venetian connections were always strong) and south to Rome and, eventually, Naples.

CHAPTER IX

❦

Epilogue

AROUND 1600, the sources of the principal styles of the early baroque period, both in sacred and secular music, were to be found in northern Italy. Rome had lost one of its greatest composers, Palestrina, a few years earlier, and Giovanni Gabrieli and Monteverdi were the influential names; their musical art was a yardstick by which the achievements of composers in other European countries might be measured. North Italian influence readily spread to the Imperial territories immediately north of the Alps; the close cultural ties between the Veneto and Austria were confirmed by the dedication to Austrian princes of several volumes of church music printed in Venice,[1] and the strong Italian presence among the musicians at the court in Graz.[2] These ties linked northern Italy with the whole of German-speaking Europe. The major German figures of the day, Hassler and Praetorius, were ardent imitators of the Venetian style (though the latter's practical suggestions – in his *Syntagma musicum* – for building a church ensemble were extravagant, tailored to the German love of wind instruments, when compared to Italian practices). The Italian influence extended even further than Germany; Giovanni Gabrieli's music was popular in Sweden and Poland, and several Danish composers came to Venice to study with him.[3] Meanwhile, a number of Italian composers with ambition cast their eyes northwards in search of good court posts in those parts of Europe.

In observing the period of transition in north Italian church music in Chapter IV, we saw how church style was changing during the last two decades of the sixteenth century. Even Palestrina espoused modern tendencies by abandoning the emphasis on linear writing. The spiritual madrigal, both in Rome and the north, was a manifestation of the positive devotional spirit of the Counter-Reformation. In Venice, the polychoral motet of the Gabrielis contained the roots of the grand concertato manner. Combined with new currents in secular music and the arrival of the concept of *basso continuo*, these developments blossomed during the first twenty years of the seventeenth century into the *stile moderno*.

By the year 1650, there were scarcely any important sacred composers in the whole of Italy except for Carissimi and Cavalli. The explanation of the apparent decline in the quantity and quality of Italian sacred music lies partly in the way historians have viewed baroque sacred music as a whole. After 1650, it is the Lutheran tradition rather than the Catholic that has been given disproportionate attention, both as a result of well-entrenched German scholarship and because the Lutheran development led up to Bach; in reality the mid- and late-baroque Italian repertory of liturgical music (as opposed to oratorio) is still comparatively uncharted. But another factor that diminished the importance of Italian church music was the very historical event which strengthened the Lutheran tradition – the end of the Thirty Years' War in 1648. Protestantism emerged fortified from battle, and there was a new upsurge of religious spirit in Germany which deepened the differences between the divided Churches. This Germanic fervour is reflected in the later works of Schütz. Like those of his fellow Germans Schein and Scheidt, Schütz's early works owed much to the Italian style, which he had been able to experience at first hand on his two visits to Venice. In 1609–12 it was the music of his teacher Giovanni Gabrieli that impressed him most, while, if the contents of his 1629 *Symphoniae sacrae* are any guide, on the second occasion (1628–9) he came under the stylistic influence of Grandi's small-scale motets with violins. Like Schein and Scheidt, Schütz transformed his style into something more austere and German in his later years, when the Thirty Years' War was over, and German Protestantism was more forceful; this change is demonstrated in his Passions and oratorios. Although his music as a whole forms the basis of a convenient link between the Catholic and Protestant traditions, this cleavage of style between his early and late works is another reflection of Italy's loss of supremacy in sacred music.

In what ways had the background to liturgical music in northern Italy changed by mid-century? With the fall in the output of new music on the part of church composers, music publishing – an ever-growing industry in Venice from the days of Petrucci until 1630 or so – faltered. It had been dealt a body-blow by the plague of 1630, and never recovered its former strength. After the plague, only the firm of Vincenti maintained a fairly steady business in church music, but even then their stock catalogue of 1649 showed how new collections had fallen off in number; many publications from the first three decades of the century were still available.

The rise of opera was, of course, one of the main factors behind the decline of composition for the liturgy. Earlier in the century, few church composers concerned themselves with opera, which was still a preserve of courts, or, in a learned city like Bologna, of academies (Girolamo Giacobbi, *maestro* at S. Petronio, wrote operas for the delight of such intellectual gatherings). But by mid-century, opera had become the dominant force: it was now a commercial activity, with public opera houses. The citizens, whose only previous contact with great music had been in church on Sundays and feast days, could now attend the spectacle of opera, run on an economically viable basis, and therefore tailored to satisfy their tastes. Venice's first public opera-house was opened in 1637, and Bologna's in 1639. Venice saw the opening of additional theatres at SS. Giovanni e Paolo in 1639, and at S.

Moisé in 1640: the first production in the latter was Monteverdi's *Arianna*. The Teatro Novissimo was opened in 1641, and Giovanni Rovetta's *Ercole in Lidia* produced; the building was destroyed by fire in 1647. By 1661 three more Venetian theatres had opened, at SS. Apostoli, S. Apollinare, and S. Salvatore.[4] In the 1640s, Monteverdi and Rovetta were the first composers who, as *maestri* at St. Mark's, turned their hands to the writing of opera for the public theatres of Venice and, in a few decades' time, this was a normal activity for the *maestro*. St. Mark's now became one of the few church posts held by composers of any significance in the field of church music, yet the incumbents obviously found the writing of opera a more attractive proposition. For a well-known *maestro* the fee for one opera could be in the 200–400 ducat range – as high as a whole year's salary in his church post.[5] Cavalli, Pietro Ziani, and Legrenzi, the successful Venetian opera composers of their day, were all employed by St. Mark's. This latter employment granted them the stable income necessary to back up their operatic activities in Venice, so much so that Ziani, failing to get Cavalli's post on the latter's death in 1676, and seeing that he would therefore be less financially secure, left for Naples.

Besides Venice and Bologna, it was the cities that had been associated with courts which now had public opera-houses: Parma, Modena, and Ferrara. In the main, Venetian, not locally composed, opera was produced in these establishments, whereas in the case of church music earlier in the century, much was written for the local cathedral by its own choirmaster. Nevertheless, the few major church composers there were outside Venice in mid-century could be found in centres where opera-houses had opened: Cazzati at Bologna, and Legrenzi at Ferrara (where he produced his first three operas in the early 1660s). The rise of opera resulted in a great increase of professionalism and virtuosity among musicians. The best singers found operatic work more attractive than church employment. The era of Viadana and of the average, unambitious small choir, for which so much early concertato music had been written, had passed – in the places where church music still flourished, competition from opera meant that standards had to be higher. Full choirs of mainly church-trained singers, able to perform in any number up to six parts, gave way to a mixed body of voices and strings. In opera, too, the chorus now played a less important part than formerly; though crowd scenes multiplied, actual chorus work decreased. The reasons were economic: just as many churches in the early years of the century had found themselves unable to support large choirs capable of performing Palestrina, so now those who ran the opera houses found that their audiences preferred solo numbers and arias, and that the money expended on a chorus and its trainer was best transferred to other purposes.[6]

Parallel with the rise of opera in northern Italy was the development of instrumental music there. In church this tended to overshadow vocal liturgical music, yet another reason for the latter's decline. Extra-liturgical music no longer consisted of motets on a relevant text, but of instrumental sonatas. With the increasing popularity of the violin family, the church string orchestra assumed an ever more significant role, and at Bologna, the centre of instrumental composition, it became the glory of music at S. Petronio. Just as Cavalli represented the new type of church composer who turned to opera as a source of fame, so Corelli later was the archetype of the church musician as instrumental virtuoso. Venice and Bologna were the two cities with the major church appointments, and yet they were not primarily centres of liturgical composition; they were the home of opera and instrumental music written by church musicians. The two developments were linked, for many composers worked in both media: Cavalli, Legrenzi, and several of the Bolognese school – Cazzati, Domenico Gabrielli, Perti and Vitali. Only one aspect of the European scene had not changed since the beginning of the century; the Italians were still dominant, though now in operatic and instrumental, rather than liturgical music. They were still emigrating north to influential positions in the Germanic lands: Cesti went to Innsbruck, others to Hanover, Dresden, and Brunswick. It was in the field of church music that the Germans, having adopted the best of the Italian manner early in the century, continued with their indigenous development of the cantata, *historia*, and oratorio.

In Italian liturgical music as a whole there occurred, around the middle of the seventeenth century, a polarization, on the one hand, towards small-scale music affected by these operatic and instrumental developments in northern Italy, and on the other towards the 'colossal Baroque' manner, which flourished in the triumphal religious climate of Rome.[7] This was a development of the old *cori spezzati*, which persisted in Rome long after it had been largely overtaken in the North by the mixed concertato style. In the middle of the seventeenth century one could go to St. Peter's, in Rome, and hear Masses by Carissimi or Benevoli in nine, ten, and even sixteen parts, in which the massive Amen chorus at the end of the Credo might last as long as a whole Sanctus.[8] Music for larger vocal textures was still one feature of the Roman musical scene, as it had been from the days of Palestrina; there was no rise of public opera or instrumental music to displace it, and it had close connections with oratorio. Unlike opera, where the chorus became less and less important, oratorio afforded splendid opportunities for dramatic choral writing which Carissimi did not fail to seize; the choruses contain some of the most notable moments in his oratorios.

In the other direction, the trend in Italian church music was towards mixed vocal and instrumental scorings. As was pointed out earlier, the only surviving form that did not involve instrumental participation was the small-scale motet for one to three voices with organ. With the rise of opera in which solo and duet numbers played an increasingly important part, writing for this medium was a common experience of both the church and the opera composer, who were well acquainted with the problems it presented. The motet for four or more voices was now much rarer, having less relation to opera; its place had been taken by works for a few voices and obbligato strings. Whereas, in the early days of the concertato style, the essential contrast inherent in the label had been that between solo and tutti, now it was that between solo voices and instruments. The musical function of the full choir had been taken over by the instrumental body as the style of string writing became more varied and idiomatic. A string ritornello was now the principal feature in a musical design, whereas before it had simply lent shape to a work that also contained vocal refrains or linked material. With the greater interest in string writing, composers were freed from the necessity of concentrating on word setting to sustain musical inspiration. The general vogue for including obbligato violins in church music is shown by the fact that, compared with Grandi's three lone 'motetti con sinfonie' publications of the 1620s, one collection with violins appeared on average every year after 1645, and this does not include large orchestral church music. The two church forms of the later baroque period, cantata and sonata, had crystallized, the frequent participation of strings in the vocal music acting as a link between them. The resources of church music, solos, duets, and trios with or without strings, were much the same as in the opera in which church composers seemed more interested.

The actual manifestations of changing musical style towards mid-century have been noted in the foregoing chapters. One point frequently made was that triple time came to be used more and more for extended paragraphs until it assumed an importance superior to that of common time. In particular, it became characterized by variety of rhythm and the melodic flow of the *bel canto* style. Vocal style was affected by idiomatic string and even keyboard writing, in the form of patterned semiquaver figurations. Greater emphasis on such vocal elaboration was parallelled by a decrease in syllabic word setting. The words seemed to be less important; certainly the Council of Trent's exhortations about intelligibility were not heeded as much as they had been fifty years earlier. Musical device often overruled textual considerations. Composers used a wider range of keys and showed a more definite sense of modulation than previously. The harmonic palette was more varied, too. The continuo bass came to be more profusely figured with 6/3 chords, 7–6 and 7–6–5 progressions; 4–3 suspensions and V–I cadences became less ubiquitous. Large-scale music became characterized by an increasing 'orderliness': for example, in Orazio Tarditi's Mass of 1648, the cantata-like triple-time episodes, with predictable modulation patterns, are dull on account of their length (the exciting chordal tuttis, reminiscent of the Venetian manner of the Gabrielis, provide a welcome relief). Much the same could be said of Cavalli's *Messa concertata* of 1656, in which the tuttis provide the most exciting sounds, the extended solo sections often tending towards graceful and innocuous padding, particularly in the Gloria and

Credo. Owing to the length of these movements, the Mass lasts fifty minutes in performance, compared with the concise and more varied music of the Grandi and Rovetta Masses, discussed earlier. Cavalli's undoubted melodic gift should be sought in his operas rather than in his sacred music.

By the mid-seventeenth century, the Counter-Reformation spirit that dominated the age of transition around 1600 had waned. Religiously and politically, Europe was a more stable place, particularly after the end of the Thirty Years' War. One might perhaps argue that the orderliness, charm, and even superficiality in, say, certain Venetian Mass settings after 1640 (Cavalli's included), was a reflection of this stability. By contrast, the music of the period 1590 to 1625 was much more directly expressive, even passionate in its fidelity to the text and to attendant human emotions. In later years, as liturgical music became more dominated by a secular spirit, this fervour was more apparent in oratorio – in the best of Carissimi or late Schütz. Deriving its dramatic force from opera, oratorio ousted liturgical music in the realm of the more intimate kinds of sacred art. Meanwhile, large-scale church music became less a manifestation of fervent Catholic aspiration than a symbol of pomp and ceremony, a backcloth for great state occasions and no more, now that the bonds between Church and state were much closer. Despite the expanding secular spirit of these later years, it is the combination of human feeling with Christian fervency in the church music of northern Italy in the early baroque period that assures it a place alongside the best work of two of the century's great names, Monteverdi and Schütz.

Notes

Introduction
1. Reprinted as an appendix to Roche, 'Duet', 44–6.

Chapter I
1. Wittkower, *Art*, 1.
2. Láng, *Civilization*, 316–19.
3. See Dixon, 'Colossal Baroque', 119.
4. Wittkower, *Art*, 3.
5. Hughes, *History*, 196 ff.
6. Fellerer, 'Trent', 576.
7. Evennett, *Counter-Reformation*, 138.
8. Lockwood, *Ruffo*.
9. Ibid., 233–5. Lockwood has edited *Seven Masses* by Ruffo (Madison, Wisconsin, 1979).
10. Lockwood, *Ruffo*, 127 ff.
11. *St. Charles Borromeo's Instructions on Ecclesiastical Buildings*, trans. G. J. Wigley (London, 1857).
12. Evennett, *Counter-Reformation*, 21–2.
13. Ibid., 40.
14. See Roche, *Palestrina*, 34, 45, 49.
15. Evennett, *Counter-Reformation*, 42.
16. Wittkower, *Art*, 4; see also Evennett, *Counter-Reformation*, 74–5.
17. Review by H. P. Cosgrove of Ganss, *St. Ignatius' Idea of a Jesuit University*, *Renaissance News*, ix (1956), 101.
18. Gradenwitz, 'Transformations', 269.
19. Culley, *Jesuits*.
20. Ibid., 16–20.
21. Ibid., 76.
22. Ibid., 88.
23. *Jesuitenorden*, 75–6, quoted in Culley, *Jesuits*, 93–4.
24. Quoted in Fellerer, 'Trent', 589.
25. Jeremias Drexel, *Rhetorica caelestis* (Antwerp, 1636), i.66, quoted in Fellerer, 'Trent'.

Chapter II
1. Bukofzer, *Baroque*, 403.
2. Arnold, 'San Rocco', 229.
3. For a fuller account of music-making there, see Roche, 'Bergamo'.
4. Belotti, *Bergamo*, iv.
5. These figures are based on the annual lists of salary confirmations in the

church-council minutes: Bergamo, Biblioteca Pubblica, *Terminationes*, Mia LXIII, vol. 36, f. 174^v; vol. 37, ff. 19, 103^v, 199; vol. 38, ff. 145^v, 245; vol. 39, f. 201.

6. For further on Bergamo, see pp. 23–4.
7. Schrade, *Monteverdi*, 269 ff.
8. Selfridge-Field, *Venetian Instrumental Music*, 27 ff; see also Arnold, 'San Rocco', and *Gabrieli*, Chapter VIII.
9. Giovanni Maria Scorzuto at Asolo was, however, lucky enough to have a solo motet published in the first-ever anthology of such works, *Ghirlanda sacra*, in 1625.
10. See especially d'Alessi, *Trevois*; and Vale, 'Udine'.
11. Tebaldini, *Padova*, 30 ff.
12. Lovato, 'Padova', 4, note 6.
13. Selfridge-Field, *Venetian Instrumental Music*, 117.
14. See Kurtzman, 'Capello'.
15. Roche, 'Bergamo' provides a fuller account.
16. Bergamo, Biblioteca Pubblica, *Spese*, Mia LXXI, vol. 4, f. 89.
17. A number of small places lying more in the centre of the *pianura padana* (whether within the Venetian Republic or not) gave employment to church composers: Salò (Giulio Cesare Monteverdi), Correggio (Giovanni Ghizzolo), Casalmaggiore (Ignazio Donati), Monselice (Antonio Gualtieri), and Mirandola (Giovanni Righi and Galeazzo Sabbatini, who both worked at the ducal chapel there).
18. McElrath, 'Donati', 36.
19. Einstein, *Madrigal*, 773.
20. Roncaglia, *Modena, passim*. On church music at Reggio Emilia, see Casali, 'Reggio'.
21. See Fenlon, 'Answers'.
22. Pelicelli, 'Parma', *NA* viii (1931), 217.
23. The papacy held sway over a number of places near Bologna and further south-east in which church composers were active: Persiceto (Ercole Porta), Imola (Banchieri), Forlì (Amante Franzoni, Orazio Tarditi), Faenza (Tarditi again), Jesi (Tarditi, Giacomo Finetti), Fano (Donati, Viadana), San Marino (Francesco Maria Marini), Pesaro (Donati again, Bartolomeo Barbarino, Lucio Billi), and Urbino (Donati, Giovanni Brunetti).
24. Sartori, 'Monteverdiana', 412–13.
25. Fedeli, *Novara, passim*.
26. Other cities within the Duchy of Milan where church composers were active included Lodi (Antonio Savetta, Donati), Como (Paolo Bottaccio, Guglielmo Lipparino), and Cremona (Tarquinio Merula).
27. This is no longer considered to be Benevoli. See Hintermaier, 'Salisburgensis'.
28. Federhofer, 'Graz', 167.
29. Reprinted in Roche, 'Inventory', 47–50.
30. These are reprinted in *MMg*, 1882–3 suppl.
31. Other publishing centres included Milan, Verona, and Ferrara.
32. For a fuller discussion of this topic, see Roche, 'Anthologies'.

Chapter III

1. Moore, *Vespers*, 185 and Table V–2, 210–13.
2. Bergamo, Biblioteca Pubblica, *Terminationes*, Mia LXIII, vol. 37, f. 268^v.
3. Ibid., Mia LXIII, vol. 38, f. 35.
4. Pelicelli, 'Parma', 217–18.

5. e.g. the Masses by Grandi (1630), Rovetta (1639), and Cazzati (1641 and 1653).
6. Bonta, 'Uses', 55–6.
7. Ibid., 61.
8. Sartori, *Bibliografia*, under 1613(a).
9. Bonta, 'Problems', 104–5.
10. Selfridge–Field, *Venetian Instrumental Music*, 24–5.
11. Ibid., 22–4.
12. These antiphons normally concluded the Office of Compline, but were to be sung at the end of Vespers whenever Compline was not to follow. This is made clear by the rubrics of the Tridentine Roman Breviary, which remained unchanged in respect of this detail until 1958.
13. Described in his *Crudities* of 1611.
14. Kurtzman, 'Perspectives', 31–3. Moore (*Vespers*, pp. 196–7) makes a distinction between adaptable collections and those which were still conceived as liturgical units in respect of the selection of psalms, the performing resources, and musical style.
15. Armstrong, 'Anerio', 89.
16. D. Stevens, preface to Monteverdi, *Vespers* (London, 1960), iii.
17. G. Biella, 'La Messa', 114.
18. This issue is fully discussed in Bonta, 'Problems'.
19. Kurtzman, 'Perspectives', 35–7.
20. Kurtzman, 'Vespers', 64–5.
21. Bonta, 'Problems', 99–100.
22. See Moore, *Vespers*, Chaptes IV and V, for a full discussion of this Office at St. Mark's, especially on the differences between the St. Mark's and Roman liturgical uses. Moore mentions (pp. 176–8) the possibility of prefacing a psalm or Magnificat with the correct chant antiphon as well as following it with an antiphon substitute, and suggests that modal concordance might simply be ignored.
23. Bergamo, Biblioteca Pubblica, *Terminationes*, Mia LXIII, vol. 38, f. 35.
24. Pelicelli, 'Parma', 218.
25. Actually only the first six verses of Psalm 30; this was dropped from the Compline psalms in the revision of the Roman Breviary carried out under Pius X in 1911.
26. See Roche, 'Compline', for further on this Office and its music. There is little evidence that other Offices were ever set to measured music except on the most infrequent basis. The Bergamo choir library possessed one volume of psalms for Terce. This Office would normally be sung only in monastic contexts, where it would immediately precede Mass. One of the very rare collections to include settings of Terce psalms, published in 1624, was by Francesco Bellazzi, who directed music at the Franciscan church in Milan.
27. Marx, 'Lamentationen', 5.
28. See Moore, *Vespers*, Table IV–6, pp. 166–9, and the discussion on pp. 148–9, concerning the correlation between Grandi's motet texts and the requirements of Vespers.
29. Soluri, 'Viadana', 99.
30. It was, of course, possible to fashion composite texts by drawing upon different parts of the liturgy of a given feast, or indeed the Commons of similar categories of feast. For example, Grandi's *Quam pulchra est* consists of words taken from a responsory from the Common of Holy Women together with the Little Chapter at None from the Common of Virgins.

31. Some of these texts were peculiar to Venice, where the liturgical traditions and practices in St. Mark's were distinct from those of the Church as a whole, and the motet could be more 'occasional' in nature.

32. Reese, *Renaissance*, 453.

33. Alaleona, 'Laudi', 1.

34. e.g. the title page of Monteverdi's Vespers collection.

35. *La Flora*, ed. K. Jeppesen (Copenhagen, 1949), ii, 7.

36. These are, of course, the normal continuo instruments for secular monody. See Fortune, 'Continuo', 10.

37. Cf. the Vespers antiphons for Virgins and Holy Women, several of which are texts from the Song of Songs. See also Moore, *Vespers*, 150–3.

Chapter IV

1. See Roche, *Palestrina*, 20–1, 28.

2. *Musica divina*, ed. K. Proske, i (Regensburg, 1853), 165.

3. Ferand, *Embellishment*. The treatises are: Girolamo della Casa, *Il vero modo di diminuir* (Venice, 1584); G. B. Bovicelli, *Regole, passaggi di musica* (Venice, 1593); Giovanni Bassano, *Ricercate passaggi et cadentie* (Venice, 1598). See also Brown, *Embellishing*.

4. Quoted in Kuhn, *Verzierungs–Kunst*, 100 ff.

5. *Musica divina*, op. cit., i. 259.

6. *Selectus novus Missarum*, ed. K. Proske, ii (Regensburg, 1861), 583.

7. L. Torchi, *L'arte musicale in Italia*. i (Milan, 1897), 445.

8. *Ten Venetian Motets*, ed. D. Arnold (London, 1980), 26.

9. *Musica divina*, op. cit., ii. 454.

10. Based on music from all three volumes of the *Cento concerti* (1602, 1607, and 1609).

11. F. T. Arnold, *Thorough–Bass*, 31.

12. Mompellio, *Viadana*, 296.

13. F. T. Arnold, *Thorough–Bass*, 25.

14. Ibid., 27.

15. See Smither, 'Dialogue', 416–17, which includes a quotation of part of this motet.

16. Mompellio, *Viadana*, 291.

17. F. T. Arnold, *Thorough–Bass*, 29.

18. Mompellio, *Viadana*, 276.

19. *Cento concerti ecclesiastici*, ed. C. Gallico (Kassel, 1964), 22.

20. Ibid., 33.

21. D. Arnold, 'Cori spezzati', 4.

22. D'Alessi, 'Precursors', 187.

23. See Carver, 'Willaert'.

24. A. Gabrieli, *Musiche da chiesa*, ed. G. d'Alessi (Milan, 1942), 48.

25. Ibid., 1.

26. See Horsley, 'Scores', 468.

27. The words 'in voce tubae' were often set in an illustrative manner: Palestrina's *Ascendit Deus* (*Opere complete*, ed. R. Casimiri, v.145, bars 25–31) has triadic trumpet figures, as do similar settings by Croce and G. Gabrieli.

28. See the motets *Domine exaudi, Deus qui beatum Marcum* and *Virtute magna*, in *Opera omnia*, ii. 62, 74, 126.

29. See Arnold, *Gabrieli*, Chapter IV.

Chapter V

1. Reprinted in *The Monody*, ed. K. G. Fellerer (Cologne, 1968), 51.
2. For further discussion and a transcription of this motet, see Roche, 'Duet', 36–7, 44–6. The motet is also ed. J. Roche (Mapa Mundi Baroque Series, London, 1982).
3. For further discussion and a transcription of this motet, see Roche, 'Duet', 38–9, 47–50. Two other duets by Grandi, *Haec est arbor* and *O sacrum convivium*, are ed. J. Roche (Mapa Mundi Baroque Series, London, 1982).
4. One reprinted in *Geschichte der Musik in Beispielen*, ed. A. Schering, p. 208; see also Smither, 'Dialogue', 424–5, and Kurtzman, 'Capello', 157–61.
5. Ed. J. Roche (Oxford Anthems Series, London, 1973). Cf. Viadana's *Filiae Jerusalem*, for SSSB; also Aurelio Signoretti's *Angelus Domini* for SSS in his first book of motets of 1615.
6. *Anfänge*, 14–15.
7. *Tutte le opere*, ed. G. F. Malipiero (Asolo, 1926–42), iv. 41.
8. As in the *Dixit Dominus* from Leoni's *Sacri fiori* of 1606. See Kurtzman, 'Perspectives', 43–7 and 55–61, where the point is made that soloistic psalm settings tend to be found in motet rather than Vespers collections.
9. Ed. J. Roche (Oxford Anthems Series, London, 1973).
10. Cf. Monteverdi's second *Laudate Dominum* from the *Selva morale* of 1641, where the opening theme and text constantly recur, giving musical coherence to the work, and also the first *Laudate pueri*: here Monteverdi tropes the opening words of the psalm into the doxology, just as Milanuzzi does in the second *Laudate pueri* of the present collection.
11. Ed. R. Ewerhart (Cantio Sacra xxiii, Cologne, 1960).
12. Sartori, *Bibliografia*.
13. For further on the sacred duet, especially Monteverdi's contribution, see Roche, 'Duet', 42–3.
14. Quoted in Gaspari, *Catalogo*, ii. 417.
15. *Tutte le opere*, xv. 606–38. Monteverdi did, of course, embrace the new medium in some of the works in his seventh book of madrigals of 1619.
16. For further on Grandi's influence on Schütz see Roche, 'Schütz'.
17. See the quotation in *The New Oxford History of Music*, v. 365.

Chapter VI

1. See Horsley, 'Scores', 477 ff.
2. Ed. J. Roche (Faber Baroque Choral Series, London, 1968).
3. Ed. J. Roche (Faber Baroque Choral Series, London, 1968).
4. Ed. F. Blume in *Drei konzertierende Motetten* (*Das Chorwerk* xl, Wolfenbüttel, 1936), p. 8.
5. See D. Arnold, 'Croce'.
6. McElrath, 'Donati', 213 ff.
7. See the quotation in *The New Oxford History of Music*, v. 351–2.
8. Ed. J. Roche (Faber Baroque Choral Series, London, 1968); other music by Priuli in *Vier Generalbassmotetten*, ed. H. J. Busch (Graz, 1970); see also Biales, 'Priuli'.
9. Ed. J. Roche (Faber Baroque Choral Series, London, 1968).
10. See the quotation in *The New Oxford History of Music*, v. 354: this illustrates the most

notable of the motet's five musical ideas, the final Alleluia, in which the tenor at one point leaps a minor ninth.

11. Ed. J. Roche (Novello, London, 1972).
12. This text is partly derived from a responsory for Assumption Day, the most solemn feast celebrated at S. Maria Maggiore in Bergamo, where Grandi was *maestro* at this time.
13. Ed. J. Roche (Oxford Anthems Series, London, 1975).
14. Reese, *Renaissance*, 491.
15. Ibid., 492, where an example of *falso bordone* is quoted, and also Kuhn, *Verzierungs–Kunst*, 142.
16. In the ensuing discussion Magnificats will be treated with psalms, for their texts are identical in format: a number of verses concluded by the doxology.
17. *Tutte le opere*, xiv. 174 and 327 respectively.
18. Ibid., xv. 418, 460 and 352 respectively. The same novel scoring as in the third *Confitebor* appears in the *Dixit Dominus* of Stefano Bernardi's *Salmi concertati* of 1637 (ed. J. Roche, Faber Baroque Choral Series, London, 1968).
19. See Roche, 'Monteverdi'.
20. For further on Rigatti see Roche, 'Rigatti'.
21. The exact meaning of 'da cappella' has recently been widely misunderstood. Praetorius (*Syntagma*, ii. 113) wrote that in Italy 'cappella' signified a choir with voices and instruments mixed, and Viadana, prefacing his polychoral psalms of 1612, asserts that unless the 'cappella' or foundation choir has at least 20 voices and instruments, it will produce a poor sound. Composers always used the term 'da cappella' in antithesis to 'concertato', implying that soloists were under no circumstances used in the former music. See also Roche, 'Prima Prattica'.
22. Published in Donfrid's anthology *Corolla Missarum* (RISM 1628²).
23. Also published in Donfrid, op. cit.
24. Two of the Masses in Bernardi's publication (one of which is the *Missa Il bianco e dolce cigno*) are reprinted in *Denkmäler der Tonkunst in Österreich*, lxix (Vienna, 1929), pp. 1 and 10.
25. See the quotation in *The New Oxford History of Music*, v. 362.
26. Other composers had used the *Aria del Gran Duca*, e.g. Banchieri in his Mass and Sonata *sopra l'Aria . . .* (1620), and his *Missa Victoria* (published in Donfrid, op. cit.); also Grandi, in the motet *Deus misereatur* for three basses (1613), and Agnelli in his psalm *Laudate Dominum* (see above pp. 102–3). See Kirkendale, *Ballo*.

Chapter VII

1. See Roche, 'Anthologies', for an account of the German editors of Italian music.
2. Kunze, 'Gabrieli', 97.
3. The Gabrieli works mentioned in this and the ensuing paragraphs are reprinted in *Opera omnia*, iii–v; in addition *In ecclesiis* is available as an Eulenburg score, ed. F. Hudson (London, 1963), and in a Novello edition, ed. D. Stevens (London, 1971); *Jubilate Deo* and *Surrexit Christus* are available in the Eulenburg Octavo Series, ed. F. Hudson (both London, 1970); and *O Jesu mi dulcissime* and *Hodie completi sunt* in *Drei Motetten*, ed. H. Besseler (Das Chorwerk x, Wolfenbüttel, 1931).
4. Winterfeld, *Gabrieli*.
5. Original Italian quoted in Mompellio, *Viadana*, 163–5.

6. A complete work from this collection, *Beatus vir*, is reprinted in Mompellio, *Viadana*, 317.

7. *Conclusioni*, appendix.

8. Kurtzman, 'Vespers', condensed in 'Perspectives'.

9. Monteverdi also used *falso bordone* in madrigals (e.g. in *Sfogava con le stelle* from Book IV) as a means of declaiming the text clearly, in accordance with new ideals in word setting.

10. 'Perspectives', 55.

11. *Civilization*, 319.

12. See Horsley, 'Scores', 471–2.

13. Moore (*Vespers*, 30–3) reproduces the list of contents of this publication, and argues that though it was issued after Grandi had left Venice for Bergamo, the selection of psalms and musical style of all the works except the second *Dixit Dominus* and Magnificat settings associate these with St. Mark's. Moore's musical appendix includes transcriptions of the *Deus in adjutorium* and *Beatus vir*.

14. Ghizzolo does occasionally use Choir II alone, and suggests that its music could be performed by instruments if wished. His preface is quoted in Sartori, *Bibliografia*, 250.

15. The musical appendix to Moore, *Vespers*, contains the *Laudate Dominum* from Grandi's *Raccolta terza*.

16. *Tutte le opere*, xv. 297. This may well have been written around 1630, though other works in the *Selva morale* were written as early as 1611; a definite chronology is difficult to establish.

17. See D. Arnold, 'Schütz's Venetian Psalms', 1071.

18. Bernardi may also have written the Mass (now lost) also performed on this occasion.

19. See Hintermaier, 'Salisburgensis'.

Chapter VIII

1. Another piece, the canticle Benedictus, does use a psalm tone cantus firmus, however. See Kurtzman, 'Perspectives', 72–3, and 'Capello', 161–2.

2. See the quotation in *The New Oxford History of Music*, v. 356.

3. Quoted in Gaspari, *Catalogo*, ii. 215–16, in the original Italian.

4. This passage is quoted in Arnold, *Monteverdi*, 161.

5. Monteverdi's *Selva morale* psalms are all reprinted in *Tutte le opere*, xv; in addition, the first *Laudate Dominum* is available as an Eulenburg score, ed. D. Arnold (London, 1966) and in Monteverdi, *Christmas Vespers*, ed. D. Stevens (London, 1979); the first *Beatus vir* is ed. J. Steele (London, 1965), the Magnificat ed. J. Steele and D. Stevens (London, 1970); *Christmas Vespers* also contains editions of the first *Laudate pueri* and the third *Confitebor*.

6. See Selfridge–Field, *Venetian Instrumental Music*, 16–17.

7. *Tutte le opere*, xvi. 231.

8. Ed. J. Roche (Novello, London, 1979). See also Roche, 'Rigatti'.

9. *Opera omnia*, iv. 116.

10. See the quotation in *The New Oxford History of Music*, v. 358–9.

11. In MS 1307 in the library of St. Michael's College, Tenbury.

12. Though the component sections are in different keys, I consider this work to be a Mass rather than a set of three 'Mass sections', partly on account of similarities of

scoring between all three sections. The lack of Sanctus and Agnus Dei is not unusual in ceremonial Masses.

13. It seems more likely that the tenor part in the Gloria was normally played on a trombone, for then the lower group would be the same in both Gloria and Credo. Not only is the part marked 'tenor or trombone', but the Gloria is headed 'a3', not 'a4', in the soloists' parts, thus omitting the tenor; and in the organ part the lower group is described in cues as 'A.Tromb.' in both Gloria and Credo. One possible reason why Grandi underlaid this part was that at the first performance one of the three Credo trombonists was playing *violin* in the Gloria (the Credo has no violin part); the fact that S. Maria Maggiore had in its employ a musician who doubled on violin and trombone supports this hypothesis. In this event, of course, the extra tenor soloist would be needed in the Gloria; he could doubtless 'warm up' for the isolated tenor solo 'Crucifixus' in the Credo.

14. *Tutte le opere*, xv. 117.
15. See the quotation in *The New Oxford History of Music*, v. 361.
16. Ed. R. Leppard (London, 1966).

Chapter IX

1. For example Aloisi, who as late as 1636 dedicated his *Contextus musicarum* to Prince Leopold Wilhelm of Austria.
2. See Federhofer, 'Graz'.
3. See Arnold, *Gabrieli*, Chapter IX.
4. Towneley Worsthorne, *Opera*, 28 ff.
5. Láng, *Civilization*, 355.
6. Towneley Worsthorne, *Opera*, 81 ff.
7. See Dixon, 'Colossal Baroque'.
8. e.g. Benevoli's *Missa Si Deus pro nobis* for four choirs.

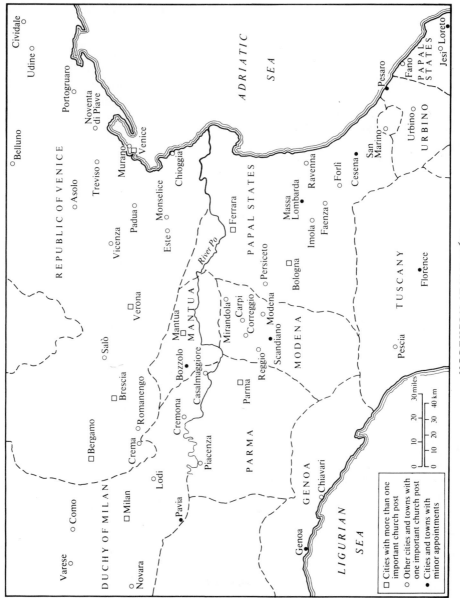

NORTHERN ITALY c1600

Cities with more than one important church post
Other cities and towns with one important church post
Cities and towns with minor appointments

ADRIATIC SEA

LIGURIAN SEA

REPUBLIC OF VENICE

DUCHY OF MILAN

PAPAL STATES

TUSCANY

MANTUA

MODENA

PARMA

GENOA

URBINO

River Po

Cividale
Udine
Belluno
Portogruaro
Noventa di Piave
Venice
Murano
Asolo
Treviso
Chioggia
Vicenza
Padua
Monselice
Este
Ferrara
Verona
Salò
Bergamo
Brescia
Crema
Romanengo
Bozzolo
Cremona
Casalmaggiore
Piacenza
Lodi
Parma
Reggio
Scandiano
Mirandola
Carpi
Correggio
Modena
Persiceto
Bologna
Massa Lombarda
Imola
Faenza
Ravenna
Forlì
Cesena
San Marino
Pesaro
Fano
Jesi
Loreto
Urbino
Florence
Pescia
Como
Varese
Novara
Pavia
Milan
Genoa
Chiavari

0   10   20   30 miles
0   20   40 km

Select Bibliography

Adrio, A., *Die Anfänge des geistlichen Konzerts* (Berlin, 1935)

Agazzari, A., *Del sonare sopra il basso* (Siena, 1607)

Alaleona, D., 'Le laudi spirituali italiane', *RMI*, xvi (1909), 1–54

Alessi, G. d', 'Precursors of Adriano Willaert in the Practice of *coro spezzato*', *JAMS*, v (1952), 187–210

—— *La cappella musicale del duomo di Treviso* (Treviso, 1954)

Armstrong, J., 'The *Antiphonae, seu sacrae cantiones* (1613) of Francesco Anerio', *AnMc*, xiv (1974) 89–150

Arnold, D., 'Giovanni Croce and the Concertato Style', *MQ*, xxxix (1953), 37–48

—— 'Alessandro Grandi, a Disciple of Monteverdi', *MQ*, xliii (1957), 171–86

—— 'Music at the Scuola di San Rocco', *ML*, xl (1959), 229–41

—— 'The Significance of "Cori Spezzati"', *ML*, xl (1959), 4–14

—— 'Music at a Venetian Confraternity in the Renaissance', *AcM*, xxxvii (1965), 62–72

—— 'Schütz's Venetian Psalms', *MT*, cxiii (1972), 1072

—— *Monteverdi* (2nd edition, London, 1975)

—— *Giovanni Gabrieli and the music of the Venetian High Renaissance* (London, 1979)

—— 'The Solo Motet in Venice (1625–1775)', *PRMA*, cvi (1979–80), 56–68

Arnold, D. and Fortune, N., *The New Monteverdi Companion* (London, 1984)

Arnold, F. T., *The Art of Accompaniment from a Thorough-Bass* (London, 1931/R1965)

Banchieri, A., *Conclusioni nel suono dell'organo* (Bologna, 1609)

—— *Cartella musicale* (Bologna, 1610)

—— *Cantorino* (Bologna, 1622)

—— *Lettere armoniche* (Bologna, 1628)

Belotti, B., *Storia di Bergamo e dei Bergamaschi* (Milan, 1959)

Biella, G., 'La Messa, il Vespro e i Sacri Concenti di Claudio Monteverdi', *Musica sacra*, 2nd Ser., ix (1964)

Biales, A., 'Giovanni Priuli's *Sacrorum Concentuum pars prima* (1618)', *AnMc*, xii (1973), 97–108

Bonta, S., 'Liturgical Problems in Monteverdi's Marian Vespers', *JAMS*, xx (1967), 87–106

—— 'The Uses of the *Sonata da Chiesa*', ibid., xxii (1969), 54–84

Brown, H. M., *Embellishing Sixteenth-century Music* (London, 1976)

Bukofzer, M., *Music in the Baroque Era* (London, 1948)

Caffi, F., *Storia della musica sacra nella già Cappella Ducale di S. Marco in Venezia dal 1318 al 1797* (Venice, 1854/R Milan, 1931)

Carver, A., 'The Psalms of Willaert and his North Italian Contemporaries', *AcM*, xlvii (1975), 270–83

Casali, G., 'La cappella musicale della cattedrale di Reggio Emilia all'epoca di Aurelio Signoretti (1567–1631)', *RIM*, viii (1973), 181–224

Coryat, T., *Coryat's Crudities* (London, 1611/R Glasgow, 1905)

Culley, T. D., *Jesuits and Music*, i (Rome, 1970)

Dixon, G., 'The Origins of the Roman "Colossal Baroque"', *PRMA*, cvi (1979–80), 115–28

—— 'Progressive Tendencies in the Roman Motet during the Early Seventeenth Century', *AcM*, liii (1981), 105–19

Einstein, A., *The Italian Madrigal* (3 vols., Princeton, 1949/R 1971)

Evennett, H. O., *The Spirit of the Counter-Reformation* (Cambridge, 1968)

Fedeli, V., *Le cappelle musicali di Novara* (Milan, 1933)

Federhofer, H., 'Graz Court Musicians', *MD*, ix (1955), 167–244

—— *Musikpflege und Musiker am Grazer Habsburgerhof* (Mainz, 1967)

Fellerer, K. G., 'Die vokale Kirchenmusik des 17/18 Jahrhunderts und die altklassische Polyphonie', *ZMw*, x (1929), 354–64

—— 'Church Music and the Council of Trent', *MQ*, xxxix (1953), 576–94

Fenlon, I., 'The Monteverdi *Vespers*: suggested answers to some fundamental questions', *Early Music*, v (1977), 380–7

Ferand, E. T., 'Didactic Embellishment Literature in the Late Renaissance: a Survey of Sources', in *Aspects of Medieval and Renaissance Music*, ed. Jan La Rue (New York, 1966), 154–72

Fortune, N., 'Italian Secular Song from 1600 to 1635: the Origins and Development of Accompanied Monody' (Unpubl. Ph.D. diss., U. of Cambridge, 1954)

—— 'Continuo Instruments in Italian Secular Monody', *GSJ*, vi (1953), 10–13

Gallico, C., 'L'arte dei "Cento Concerti Ecclesiastici" di Lodovico Viadana', in *La nuova musicologia italiana* (Turin, 1965), 55–86

Gaspari, G., *De' musicisti bolognesi nella seconda metà del sec. XVI* (Modena, 1877)

—— *Catalogo della Biblioteca Musicale G. B. Martini di Bologna* (4 vols., Bologna, 1890–1905/R 1961)

Glover, J., *Cavalli* (London, 1978)

Goldschmidt, H., *Die italienische Gesangsmethode* (Breslau, 1890)

Gradenwitz, P., 'Mid-Eighteenth-Century Transformations of Style', *ML*, xviii (1937), 265–75

Guerrini, P., 'Per la storia della musica a Brescia. Frammenti e documenti', *NA*, xi (1934), 1–28

Hintermaier, E., 'The Missa Salisburgensis', *MT*, cxvi (1975), 965–6

Hockley, N., 'Bartolomeo Barbarino e i primordi della monodia', *RIM*, vii (1972), 82–102

Horsley, I., 'Full and Short Scores in the Accompaniment of Italian Church Music in the Early Baroque', *JAMS*, xxx (1977), 466–99

Hughes, P., *A Popular History of the Catholic Church* (London, 1949)

Kenton, E. F., 'The Late Style of Giovanni Gabrieli', *MQ*, xlviii (1962), 427–43

—— *Life and Works of Giovanni Gabrieli* (Rome, 1967)

Kirkendale, W., *L'Aria di Fiorenza id est Il Ballo del Gran Duca* (Florence, 1972)

Kuhn, M., *Die Verzierungs-Kunst in der Gesangs-Musik des 16.–17. Jahrhunderts (1535–1650)* (Leipzig, 1902)

Kunze, S., 'Die Entstehung des Concertoprinzips im Spätwerk Giovanni Gabrielis', *AMw*, xxi (1964), 81–110

Kurtzman, J., 'The Monteverdi Vespers of 1610 and their relationship with Italian sacred music of the early 17th century' (Unpubl. Ph.D. diss., U. of Illinois, 1972)

—— 'Some Historical Perspectives on the Monteverdi Vespers', *AnMc*, xv (1975), 29–86

—— 'Giovanni Francesco Capello, an Avant-Gardist of the Early Seventeenth Century', *MD*, xxxi (1977), 155–82

—— *Essays on the Monteverdi Mass and Vespers of 1610*, Rice University Studies, Vol. 64, No. 4 (1978)

Láng, P. H., *Music in Western Civilization* (London, 1942)

Leichtentritt, H., *Geschichte der Motette* (Leipzig, 1908)

Lewis, A. and Fortune, N., eds., *Opera and Church Music 1630–1750*, The New Oxford History of Music, v (London, 1975)

Ligi, B., 'La cappella musicale del duomo d'Urbino', *NA*, ii (1925), 1–369

Lockwood, L., *The Counter-Reformation and the Masses of Vincenzo Ruffo* (Venice, 1970)

Lovato, A., 'Gli organisti della cattedrale di Padova nel sec. XVII', *RIM*, xvii (1982), 3–70

Mantese, G., *Storia musicale vicentina* (Vicenza, 1956)

Marx, H. J., 'Monodische Lamentationen des Seicento', *AMw*, xxviii (1971), 1–23

McElrath, H. T., 'A Study of the Motets of Ignazio Donati' (Unpubl. Ph.D. diss., U. of Rochester, 1967)

Mompellio, F., *Lodovico Viadana* (Florence, 1967)

Moore, J. H., *Vespers at St. Mark's: Music of Alessandro Grandi, Giovanni Rovetta and Francesco Cavalli* (2 vols., Ann Arbor, 1981)

—— 'The *Vespero delli Cinque Laudate* and the Role of *Salmi Spezzati* at St. Mark's', *JAMS*, xxxiv (1981), 249–78

Moser, H., *Heinrich Schütz: his Life and Work*, trans. C Pfatteicher (St. Louis, 1959)

Padoan, M., 'Tarquinio Merula nelle fonti documentarie' in *Contributi e studi di liturgia e musica nella regione padana*, 231–329

—— *La musica in S. Maria Maggiore a Bergamo nel periodo di Giovanni Cavaccio (1598–1626)* (Como, 1983)

Paganuzzi, E. and others, *La musica a Verona* (Verona, 1976)

Pelicelli, N., 'Musicisti in Parma nei secoli XV–XVI', *NA*, viii (1931), 132–42

—— 'Musicisti in Parma nel secolo XVII', *NA*, ix (1932), 112–29 and x (1933), 32–43

Praetorius, M., *Syntagma Musicum* (3 vols., Wolfenbüttel, 1619; facsimile ed., Kassel, 1958)

Redlich, H. F., 'Monteverdi's Religious Music', *ML*, xxvii (1946), 208–15

—— *Claudio Monteverdi: Life and Works* (London, 1952)

Reese, G., *Music in the Renaissance* (London, 1959)

Roche, J., 'An Inventory of Choirbooks at S. Maria Maggiore, Bergamo, January 1628', *RMARC*, v (1965), 47–50

—— 'Music at S. Maria Maggiore, Bergamo, 1614–1643', *ML*, xlvii (1966), 296–312

—— 'The Duet in Early Seventeenth-Century Italian Church Music', *PRMA*, xciii (1966–7), 33–50

—— 'North Italian Liturgical Music in the Early Seventeenth Century' (Unpubl. Ph.D. diss., U. of Cambridge, 1968)

—— 'Monteverdi and the *Prima Prattica*', in *The New Monteverdi Companion*, ed. D. Arnold and N. Fortune (London, 1984)

—— *Palestrina* (London, 1971)

—— 'Monteverdi: an Interesting Example of Second Thoughts', *MR*, xxxii (1971), 193–204

—— 'What Schütz learned from Grandi in 1629', *MT*, cxiii (1972), 1074–5

—— 'Anthologies and the Dissemination of Early Baroque Italian Sacred Music', *Soundings*, iv (1974), 6–12

—— 'Giovanni Antonio Rigatti and the Development of Venetian Church Music in the 1640s', *ML*, lvii (1976), 256–67

—— '*Musica diversa di Compietà* – Compline and its music in 17th-century Italy', *PRMA*, cix (1982–3)

Roncaglia, G., *La cappella musicale del duomo di Modena* (Florence, 1957)

Rosenthal, K., 'Steffano Bernardis Kirchenwerke', *SMw*, xv (1928), 46–61

Sander, H. A., 'Beiträge zur Geschichte der Barockmesse', *KJb*, xxviii (1933)

Sartori, C., *Bibliografia della musica strumentale italiana*, i (Florence, 1952); ii (*ivi* 1968, with corrections and additions)

—— 'Monteverdiana', *MQ*, xxviii (1952), 399–413

Schmitz, E., *Geschichte der weltlichen Solokantate* (Leipzig, 1914/R 1955)

Schrade, L., *Monteverdi: Creator of Modern Music* (London, 1950)

Scotti, C., *Il pio istituto musicale Donizetti in Bergamo* (Milan, 1901)

Selfridge, E., 'Organists at the Church of SS. Giovanni e Paolo', *ML*, l (1969), 393–9

Selfridge-Field, E., *Venetian Instrumental Music from Gabrieli to Vivaldi* (Oxford, 1975)

Smither, H., 'The Latin Dramatic Dialogue and the Nascent Oratorio', *JAMS*, xx (1967), 403–33

Soluri, J. J., 'The Concerti Ecclesiastici of Lodovico Grossi da Viadana' (Unpubl. Ph.D. diss., U. of Michigan, 1967)

Stevens, D., 'Where are the Vespers of Yesteryear?', *MQ*, xlvii (1961), 315–30

—— *Monteverdi: Sacred, Secular and Occasional Music* (London, 1978)

—— 'Monteverdi's Other Vespers', *MT*, cxx (1979), 732–7

Tagmann, P., *Archivalische Studien zur Musikpflege am Dom von Mantua* (Berne, 1967)

Tebaldini, G., *L'archivio musicale della Cappella Antoniana in Padova* (Padua, 1895)

—— *L'archivio musicale della Cappella Lauretana* (Loreto, 1921)

Towneley Worsthorne, S., *Venetian Opera in the Seventeenth Century* (Oxford, 1954 /R 1968)

Vale, G., 'La cappella musicale del duomo di Udine', *NA*, vii (1930), 87–201

Virgili, L., 'La cappella musicale della chiesa metropolitana di Fermo', *NA*, vii (1930), 1–86

Whenham, J., *Duet and Dialogue in the Age of Monteverdi* (2 vols., Ann Arbor, 1982)

Winter, P., *Der mehrchörige Stil* (Frankfurt, 1964)

Winterfeld, C. von, *Johannes Gabrieli und sein Zeitalter* (Berlin, 1834)

Wittkower, R., *Art and Architecture in Italy 1600–1750* (London, 1958)

Wittwer, M., *Die Musikpflege im Jesuitorden unter besonderer Berücksichtigung der Länder deutscher Zunge* (Greifswald, 1934)

Witzenmann, W., 'Die italienische Kirchenmusik des Barocks: ein Bericht über die Literatur aus den Jahren 1945 bis 1974', *AcM*, xlviii (1976), 77–103

Woodworth, G. W., 'Texture versus Mass in the Music of Giovanni Gabrieli', in *Essays on Music in Honor of A. T. Davison* (Cambridge, Mass., 1957), 129–38

Music in Original Printed Sources

✑ ✑ ✑ ✑

THIS is not intended to be an exhaustive catalogue of source material; it lists publications mentioned in the body of the text, or consulted in its preparation. All items were printed at Venice except where otherwise stated; an 'R' before the date of publication denotes a reprint, where the first edition is no longer extant. Each single-composer entry ends with the relevant identification mark in the RISM *Einzeldrücke* series. Anthologies are listed chronologically at the end and labelled by the RISM numbers used in the text.

Agnelli, Lorenzo. *Salmi e messa*, 1637. A399.
Aloisi, Giovanni Battista. *Coelestis parnassus*, 1628. A872.
— *Harmonicum coelum . . . missae*, 1628. A875.
— *Contextus musicarum*, 1637. A876.
Assandra, Caterina. *Motetti*, Milan, 1609. A2637.
Bacilieri, Giovanni. *Lamentationes, Benedictus et Evangelia*, 1607. B564.
Banchieri, Adriano. *Concerti ecclesiastici*, 1595. B799.
— *Ecclesiastiche sinfonie*, 1607. B802.
— *Primo libro delle messe e motetti*, 1620. B811.
— *L'organo suonarino*, 1605. B841.
Barbarino, Bartolomeo. *Il primo libro de mottetti . . . una voce*, 1610. B873.
— *Il secondo libro delli motetti . . . una voce*, 1614. B874.
Bartolini, Orindio. *Compietà con le littanie*, 1613. B1143.
— *Messe concertate a 8 voci e messa per li morti* 1633. B1144.
Bellanda, Lodovico. *Sacre laudi*, 1613. B1711.
Bellazzi, Francesco. *Psalmi ad vesperas*, 1618. B1719.
— *Messa, motetti, letanie*, 1622. B1721.
— *Salmi concertati all'uso moderno*, 1624. B1723.
Bernardi, Stefano. *Psalmi integri*, 1613. B2044.
— *Messe, parte sono per capella, e parte per concerto*, 1615. B2051.
— *Salmi concertati*, 1637. B2061.
Bianchi, Andrea. *Motetti, e messe a 8 voci*, 1611. B2497.
Billi, Lucio. *Messa e motetti a 8 voci*, 1601. B2643.
Bona, Valerio. *Messa e vespro*, 1611. B3433.
Bonachelli, Giovanni. *Corona di sacri gigli*, 1642. B3440.
Borsaro, Arcangelo. *Sacri sacrificii per gli defonti*, 1608. B3780.
— *Odorati fiori*, 1615. B3782.
Bruschi, Giulio. *Missa, et psalmi*, 1627. B4832.

Burlini, Antonio. *Riviera fiorita*, 1612. B5022.
— *Salmi intieri*, 1613. B5023.
Busatti, Cherubino. *Compago ecclesiasticorum motectorum*, 1640. B5100.
Capello, Giovanni Francesco. *Sacrorum concentuum*, 1610. C902.
— *Lamentationi, Benedictus e Miserere*, Verona, 1612. C903.
— *Motetti et dialoghi*, 1615. C906.
Capilupi, Gemignano. *Motectorum 6 et 8 vocibus, liber primus*, 1603. C909.
Caprioli, Giovanni Paolo. *Sacrae cantiones*, Modena, 1618. C944.
Casati, Gasparo. *Il primo libro de motetti*, 1643. C1411.
— *Il terzo libro de sacri concenti*, 1640. C1404.
— *Scielta d'ariosi salmi*, 1645. C1420.
Cavaccio, Giovanni. *Musica concordia*, 1620. C1554.
Cazzati, Maurizio. *Salmi e messa*, 1641. C1577.
Ceresini, Giovanni. *Il primo libro di motetti*, 1617. C1696.
Chinelli, Giovanni Battista. *Il primo libro di motetti a voce sola*, 1637. C2060.
— *Compietà, antifone, e letanie*, 1639. C2062.
— *Il secondo libro delle messe concertate*, 1648. C2064.
Cima, Giovanni Paolo. *Concerti ecclesiastici*, Milan, 1610. C2229.
Cornetti, Paolo, *Motetti concertati*, 1638. C3948.
Crivelli, Giovanni Battista. *Il primo libro delli motetti concertati*, 1626. C4421.
Croatti, Francesco. *Messa e motetti*, 1608. C4426.
Croce, Giovanni. *Sacre cantilene concertate*, 1610. C4463.
Crotti, Arcangelo. *Il primo libro de' concerti ecclesiastici*, 1608. C4552.
Donati, Ignazio. *Motetti . . . in concerto*, 1616. D3380.

— *Concerti ecclesiastici a 2–5 voci*, 1618. D3383.
— *Concerti ecclesiastici a 1–4 voci*, 1618. D3387.
— *Motetti concertati*, 1618. D3391.
— *Messe . . . parte da capella, e da concerto*, 1622. D3393.
— *Salmi boscarecci concertati*, 1623. D3396.
— *Il secondo libro de motetti a voce sola*, 1636. D3403.
Fergusio, Giovanni Battista. *Motetti e dialoghi*, 1612. F249.
Finetti, Giacomo. *Omnia in nocte Nativitatis Domini*, 1609. F812.
— *Psalmi ad vesperas*, 1611. F813.
Fontei, Nicolò. *Melodiae sacrae*, 1637. F1487.
— *Messa, e salmi*, 1647. F1490.
Franzoni, Amante. *Apparato musicale*, 1613. F1813.
Freddi, Amadio. *Messa, vespro e compietà*, 1616. F1829.
— *Psalmi integri*, 1626. F1832.
Gabrieli, Giovanni. *Sacrae symphoniae*, 1597. G86.
— *Symphoniae sacrae . . . liber secundus*, 1615. G87.
Gallerano, Leandro. *Ecclesiastica armonia*, 1624. G156.
— *Messa e salmi concertati*, 1629. G160.
Ganassi, Giacomo. *Ecclesiastici missarum*, 1634. G323.
Ghizzolo, Giovanni. *Concerti all'uso moderno*, Milan, 1611. G1783.
— *Messe, motetti, Magnificat*, Milan, 1613. G1786.
— *Messa, salmi, lettanie*, 1619. G1791.
— *Salmi, messa e falsi bordoni*, 1620. G1792.
Giacobbi, Girolamo. *Prima parte dei salmi concertati*, 1609. G1821.
Girelli, Santino. *Salmi brevi di tutto l'anno*, 1620. G2513.
Grandi, Alessandro. *Il primo libro de motetti*, 1610. G3417.
— *Il secondo libro de motetti*, 1613. G3422.
— *Motetti a 5 voci*, Ferrara, 1614. G3427.
— *Il terzo libro de motetti*, R1618. G3436.
— *Il quarto libro de motetti*, 1616. G3431.
— *Celesti fiori . . . libro V*, 1619. G3439.
— *Motetti a voce sola*, 1621. G3443.
— *Motetti a 1 et 2 voci con sinfonie d'istromenti*, 1621. G3445.
— *Motetti . . . con sinfonie . . . libro II*, R1625. G3448.
— *Motetti . . . con sonfonie . . . libro III*, 1629. G3450.
— *Salmi brevi*, 1629. G3453.
— *Messa, e salmi*, 1630. G3458.
— *Raccolta terza . . . de messa et salmi*, 1630. G3460.
— *Il sesto libro de motetti*, 1630. G3455.

Grillo, Giovanni Battista. *Sacri concentus*, 1618. G4620.
Gualtieri, Alessandro. *Motetti . . . libro II*, 1616. G4789.
Gualtieri, Antonio. *Il secondo libro de mottetti*, 1612. G4792.
— *Mottetti . . . libro III*, 1630. G4793.
Lappi, Pietro. *Missarum . . . liber I*, 1613. L685.
— *Compietà a 3 e 4 chori*, 1626. L692.
— *Hymni per tutto l'anno*, 1628. L698.
Lazari, Alberto. *Armonie spirituali*, 1637. L1182.
Leoni, Leone. *Sacri fiori*, 1606. L1997.
— *Omnium solemnitatum psalmodia*, 1613. L2008.
Marini, Francesco Maria. *Concerti spirituali*, 1637. M672.
Massaino, Tiburzio. *Musica per cantare*, 1607. M1286.
Merula, Tarquinio. *Libro secondo de concerti spirituali*, 1628. M2339.
— *Concerto . . . messi, salmi . . . concertati*, 1639. M2340.
— *Pegaso . . . salmi, motetti, suonate*, R1640. M2341.
— *Arpa Davidica*, 1640. M2342.
Milani, Francesco. *Letanie e motetti*, 1638. M2729.
Milanuzzi, Carlo. *Concerto sacro di salmi intieri*, 1627. M2746.
— *Messe a 3 concertate*, 1629. M2750.
— *Hortus sacer deliciarum*, 1636. M2754.
Milleville, Francesco (Barnaba). *Il secondo libro delle messe*, 1617. M2805.
Monteverdi, Claudio. *Sanctissimae virgini missa . . . ac vespere*, 1610. M3445.
— *Selva morale e spirituale*, 1641. M3446.
— *Messa et salmi*, 1650. M3447.
Moro, Giacomo. *Concerti ecclesiastici*, 1604. M3732.
Mortaro, Antonio. *Partitio sacrarum cantionum*, Milan, 1598. M3738.
— *Messa, salmi, motetti, et Magnificat a 3 chori*, Milan, 1599. M3741.
Negri, Marc'Antonio. *Primo libro delli salmi*, 1613. N364.
Nodari, Giovanni Paolo. *Harmonicum concentum*, 1620. N734.
Pace, Pietro. *Il primo libro de motetti*, 1613. P3.
— *Il sesto libro de motetti*, 1618. P9.
— *Motetti*, 1619. P10.
Pallavicino, Benedetto. *Sacrae Dei laudes*, 1605. P771.
Patta, Serafino. *Sacrorum canticorum*, 1613. P1038.
— *Motetti et madrigali*, 1614. P1039.
Porta, Ercole. *Sacro convito musicale*, 1620. P5194.
Priuli, Giovanni. *Sacrorum concentuum . . . pars I*, 1618. P5476.

— *Sacrorum concentuum . . . pars altera*, 1619.
P5477.

Puliti, Gabriello. *Il secondo libro delle messe*, 1620.
P5658.

Rigatti, Giovanni Antonio. *Primo parto de motetti*, 1634. R1411.

— *Messa e salmi*, 1640. R1413.

— *Messa e salmi ariosi*, R1643. R1414.

— *Salmi diversi di compietà*, 1646. R1417.

— *Motetti a voce sola . . . libro II*, 1647.
R1419.

— *Messa e salmi . . . libro II*, 1648. R1420.

Rovetta, Giovanni. *Salmi concertati*, 1626.
R2962.

— *Motetti concertati*, 1635. R2964.

— *Messa, e salmi concertati*, 1639. R2966.

— *Salmi*, 1644. R2972.

Santa Maria, Salvatore. *Sacrorum concentuum . . . libro I*, 1620. S889.

Signoretti, Aurelio. *Il primo libro de motetti*,
1615. S3424.

— *Vespertinae omnium solemnitatum psalmodiae*,
1629. S3425.

Stefanini, Giovanni Battista. *Motetti liber I*,
1604. S4727.

Tarditi, Orazio. *Celesti fiori*, 1629. T186.

— *Messe . . . in concerto*, 1639. T191.

— *Concerto il XVIII: musiche da chiesa*, 1641.
T194.

— *Messe*, 1648. T201.

Tomasi, Biagio. *Quaranta concerti*, 1615. T921.

Tonnolini, Giovanni Battista. *Salmi a 8 voci*,
1616. T960.

Tresti, Flaminio. *Messe a 5 voci libro I*, 1613.
T1177.

Turini, Francesco. *Motetti a voce sola*, Brescia,
1629. T1392.

— *Messe da cappella*, 1643. T1395.

Usper, Francesco. *Messa, e salmi . . . sinfonie, et motetti*, 1614. U116.

Vernizzi, Ottavio. *Caelestium applausus*, 1612.
V1296.

Viadana, Lodovico. *Cento concerti ecclesiastici*,
1602. V1360.

— *Completorium romanum*, 1606. V1379.

— *Concerti ecclesiastici, libro secondo*, 1607.
V1380.

— *Il terzo libro de' concerti ecclesiastici*, 1609.
V1392.

— *Salmi . . . a 4 chori*, 1612. V1400.

Villani, Gasparo. *Psalmi omnes . . . libro terzo*,
1610. V1552.

1608[13] *Concerti*, Milan, 1608. Ed. Francesco
Lucino.

1611[1] *Promptuarii musici*, i, Strasbourg, 1611.
Ed. Abraham Schadaeus.

1615[2] *Reliquiae sacrorum concentuum*, Nürnberg,
1615. Ed. Georg Gruber.

1615[13] *Parnassus musicus Ferdinandeus*, 1615. Ed.
G. B. Bonometti.

1617[2] *Seconda aggiunta alli concerti*. Milan, 1617.
Ed. Francesco Lucino.

1620[2] *Symbolae diversorum musicorum*, 1620. Ed.
Lorenzo Calvi.

1624[2] *Seconda raccolta de' sacri canti*, 1624. Ed.
Lorenzo Calvi.

1625[2] *Ghirlanda sacra*, 1625. Ed. Leonardo
Simonetti.

1626[3] *Rosarium litaniarum*, 1626. Ed. Lorenzo
Calvi.

1626[5] *Flores praestantissimorum virorum*, Milan,
1626. Ed. Filippo Lomazzo.

1628[2] *Corolla musica*, Strasbourg, 1628. Ed.
Johann Donfrid.

1629[5] *Quarta raccolta de' sacri canti*, 1629. Ed.
Lorenzo Calvi.

Index

Index of Musical Examples

❧

Much recent writing on Italian church music of the early Baroque has centred on Venice and her illustrious composers Giovanni Gabrieli and Monteverdi. But Venice was only one amongst a host of north Italian cities that nurtured the growth of church music, and gave employment to many composers of talent. Venice's importance was as publishing centre for a vast repertory of new music which received wide dissemination, effectively reaching a wider public than either opera or madrigal. This book aims to provide a very necessary, and long overdue, sense of perspective against which we can view the position of Venice and the achievements of her major figures during a time when music was experiencing volatile change and stylistic experiment.

The 'age of Monteverdi' in the title encompasses the period of his mature working life—from about 1605 until 1643. His own works represent a microcosm of the vast range of styles and textures that we find in the sacred music of the time, from the simple solo motet with continuo to brilliant and sonorous works for special Venetian occasions like the seven-part *Gloria*. But only if it is considered against a fuller background than has ever been attempted before does it become clear that Monteverdi's sacred music, rather than leading and forming musical taste, often in fact responded to it, and that a number of colleagues and contemporaries were equally important in developing new forms, idioms and scorings in their sacred music. Moreover this music was often excellent; its qualities are illustrated (necessarily, in view of the dearth of published modern editions) by numerous musical examples throughout those chapters which concern matters of style.